The Short Guide Series

UNDER THE EDITORSHIP OF

Sylvan Barnet

Marcia Stubbs

A Short Guide to Writing about Literature by Sylvan Barnet

A Short Guide to Writing about Art by Sylvan Barnet

A Short Guide to Writing about Biology by Jan A. Pechenik

A Short Guide to Writing about Social Science by Lee J. Cuba

*A Short Guide
to Writing
about Social
Science*

A Short Guide to Writing about Social Science

LEE J. CUBA
Wellesley College

Scott, Foresman/Little, Brown College Division
Scott, Foresman and Company
Glenview, Illinois Boston London

Library of Congress Cataloging-in-Publication Data

Cuba, Lee J.
  A short guide to writing about social science.

  (The Short guide series)
  Includes index.
  1. Social sciences—Authorship. 2. English
language—Technical English. I. Title.
H91.C78 1987   808'.0663   87–27503
ISBN 0–673–39766–1

  2 3 4 5 6 7 8 9 10 — KPF — 93 92 91 90 89 88

Printed in the United States of America

Acknowledgments
Pages 8–9: From Lee Cuba, "Reorientations of Self: Residential Identification in Anchorage, Alaska," in *Studies in Symbolic Interaction,* Vol. 5, 1985,
pp. 222–223, JAI Press, Inc., Greenwich, CT. Reprinted by permission.

Page 17: From Miriam J. Wells, "The Resurgence of Sharecropping: Historical Anomaly or Political Strategy?" *American Journal of Sociology* 90(1), 1984.
Copyright © 1984 by The University of Chicago. All rights reserved. Reprinted by permission of The University of Chicago Press.

Page 17: Annotation of Richard A. Epstein's *Takings: Private Property and
the Power of Eminent Domain, American Bar Foundation Journal,* No. 4, 1985,
p. 972. Copyright © 1986 by the American Bar Foundation Journal. Reprinted by permission.

Pages 21–22: Student book review. Reprinted by permission of Elizabeth L.
Stone.

Pages 23–24: From Gerald N. Grob's review of David J. Rothman's *The
Discovery of the Asylum, Political Science Quarterly* 87:325–326, 1972. Re-
printed by permission of The Academy of Political Science, 2852 Broadway,
New York, NY.

Page 32: From Joanne Miller and Howard H. Garrison, "Sex Roles: The
Division of Labor in the Workplace," *Annual Review of Sociology* 8:237, 1982.
Copyright © 1982 by Annual Reviews, Inc. Reprinted by permission.

(continued on page 164)

to Kai Erikson
friend, teacher, and master of the craft of writing

Preface

As teachers of social science, instructors tell their students to question the taken-for-granted world and to challenge the assumptions that are the foundation of everyday life. They do this so that their students might come to see the world in a new way or discover that, on closer inspection, things are not always as they seem. Ironically, these same teachers adopt quite the opposite approach when it comes to student writing: they assume that their students know how to write a book review, a library research paper, or a short fieldwork assignment. When the required paper appears on their desks, they soon discover their mistake, but a host of factors—lack of time, the number of papers, or perhaps even their own perceived inadequacies as teachers of writing—may prevent them from addressing the problem. Frustrated and wishing they had the time to edit each paper closely, they begin marking the next one.

In this book on writing about social science, I have tried to take little for granted in the hope that it will give students a clearer idea of what their instructors are asking them to do when written work is assigned. The book can supplement any social science course, but it should be particularly useful to students enrolled in courses in which research papers are assigned. Each chapter is self-contained so that instructors can assign a particular chapter or section without further comment. The book is brief and is designed to be used as a convenient reference that will not add substantially to the amount of required reading for any course.

Chapter 1, The Practice of Writing, discusses writing as a recursive process that involves taking notes, making drafts, rethinking, and revising. Using an example from my own writing, I illustrate how analytic insights can emerge through this process and offer some suggestions on how to develop an effective strategy for writing. This chapter, read with Chapter 8, Revising, should be helpful to all students regardless of the type of writing they are asked to do.

Chapters 2 through 5 focus on specific types of social science writing that are often a part of both undergraduate and graduate curriculums. Chapter 2 discusses abstracts and other summaries, book reviews, and reviews of the literature, moving from writing that is primarily descriptive to that which is more analytical and critical. I suggest how to read social science research with an eye toward summary and offer ways of organizing summaries into a longer review. Chapter 3, the longest in the book, deals with papers based on original research. Following the format used in professional journal writing, I discuss each part of the research paper and point out several approaches to presenting qualitative and quantitative data. Undergraduates enrolled in research methods courses or intensive research seminars, or graduate students preparing papers for publication should find this chapter particularly useful. In Chapter 4, Library Research Papers, I describe how to select a topic and organize papers based solely on secondary source materials, with special attention to issues of outlining and balance. Chapter 5 offers several suggestions for lessening the anxiety that often accompanies two of the most stressful yet potentially rewarding occasions in studying social science: oral presentations and essay examinations.

Chapter 6, Using the Library, and Chapter 7, Form, are included as basic reference sources for any type of social science writing. I describe library materials that address a broad range of social science concerns, and present detailed information on how to use specialized indexes, such as the *Social Science Citation Index*. In the chapter on form, I discuss several skills that instructors frequently assume their students know, including when and how to quote materials or use footnotes, how to make citations within the text, and how to compile a list of references. I also include some words of caution about plagiarism and sexist language.

I have been fortunate to have found myself in various settings where writing was talked about seriously. As a member of the writing seminar directed by Kai Erikson at Yale University and as an instructor in the writing program at Wellesley College, I have had an opportunity to reflect on my own writing and to discuss the practice of writing with both students and colleagues. Under the guidance of Sylvan Barnet and Marcia Stubbs, editors of this volume, I have been a student of two master teachers of writing. I could not have hoped for more insightful or inspiring critics.

For comments that have enriched both the style and substance of this book, I thank Kathryn Lynch, Diane Pike, Susan Silbey, and Diane Vaughan. I owe a special debt to Joan Stockard for her significant contributions to Chapter 6. The staff at Little, Brown—in particular, Cynthia Chapin, Amy Johnson, Joe Opiela, Carolyn Potts, and Nan Upin—made the transition from manuscript to book relatively painless; Editing, Design & Production attentively supervised the copyediting and typesetting of the book. As always, I have profited from an ongoing dialogue with Patricia Ewick, the most generous colleague and gifted teacher I know.

Contents

*A Short Guide
to Writing
about Social
Science*

1
The Practice of Writing

Social scientists write about the methods they use to collect and analyze social data, and they write about the results these methods yield. But social scientists have seldom examined the practice of writing itself. As a result, students in the social sciences see little of what happens between the collection of data and publication of the research results. *A Short Guide to Writing About Social Science* focuses on this critical omission by taking a serious look at the practice of social science writing.

Effective writing—about any subject—requires practice. In one sense (as in "practice makes perfect"), practice means repeated writing, editing and rewriting, sharpening words so that we express our ideas clearly to our audience. But writing can also be thought of as a practice in a different sense (as in "medical practice"), as a complex of routines we develop around the act of writing. These routines reflect our assumptions about the nature of creative thought, as well as our superstitions about our own success or failure as writers. For instance, many undergraduates believe that writing a term paper is a task composed of a series of discrete steps: one chooses a topic, then compiles a bibliography, collects data, organizes the paper, and finally writes the paper. In such a model, writing begins only *after* all of the necessary research is done and the argument is well organized. The actual writing of the paper, according to this perspective, involves nothing more than communicating what already exists "in our mind." Creativity enters into this process only in deciding *how* to say what we have discovered, not in determining *what* to say.

1

Students who hold this misconception about the writing process often put off writing until the paper is fully outlined and developed—or until time has run out and the due date is approaching. Inadequacies or shortcomings of the paper are, therefore, typically attributed to insufficient time. The irony of conceiving of writing as the grand conclusion to weeks of research is that it serves as a deterrent to writing in the first place. Thinking that we must know exactly what we are going to say before we begin writing can create a "writer's block" of seemingly insurmountable proportions.

Defining writing as simply communicating ideas to *others* fails to take into account that, in writing, we communicate something *to ourselves*. When we write a paper or even a sentence, we *objectify* our thoughts. Through writing, our thoughts are separated from us, assuming an existence and a nature of their own. You have no doubt experienced this process yourself, although you may not have thought of it in these terms. Have you ever reread a paper or a letter you wrote months or years ago? If you have, you may have been amazed that what you were reading was written by you. And depending on what you read, your reaction may have ranged from embarrassment to pride.

My point is that in reading such a paper or letter, you are forced to confront and experience the objective reality of your words. Of course, months or years need not elapse before we come to see our writing as distinct from ourselves. The minute we write a sentence we may realize that it doesn't express what we want to say, or (even more often) that it does express what we *did have* to say but we now see we have a better idea. We write, "There are two reasons why . . . ," and our mind, racing ahead, suddenly realizes we are thinking of *three* reasons or, on the other hand, that one of our two reasons isn't much of a reason and isn't worth stating.

Thus, writing provides a constant opportunity to deepen your understanding and sharpen your insights. Taking advantage of this opportunity requires that writing be followed by revising and rewriting to reflect these insights. What we call "writing" might better be called "rewriting" or "revising." Think of writing as a process—not an outcome—involving an ongoing dialogue with yourself and with your other imagined readers. As you organize observations, fashion arguments, and articulate conclusions, new ideas will emerge. Writing, an analytically creative task, is a necessary part of social research. This means that writing, like the methods of social research, can help you learn more about social life.

Recognizing that writing is an analytic strategy that you can develop with practice requires that you adopt certain attitudes toward writing *as* a practice. First, this perspective on writing, I have already suggested, frees you from the burden of developing a tight-knit argument before you commit your thoughts to paper. It implies that your first draft will not (or more to the point, *cannot*) be your final product. Only after you begin to write your paper, essay, or examination will you know what you want to say, and you will almost surely find that your idea of what you want to say develops as you write it.

Taking revision to heart means that you must be willing to part with your words. It is not unusual for practiced writers to labor over a paragraph or a page, only to realize later that those carefully crafted words must be discarded. Being wedded to a single expression of your ideas not only ignores the emergent nature of writing, but it also thwarts your understanding of what you are trying to write about.

Second, viewing your words as separate from yourself helps you to accept constructive criticisms of your writing. It is easy to regard editorial criticism as a personal attack on your character, indicative of some intellectual flaw. All writers feel slightly anxious while watching someone read their work. Of course, you would welcome a little praise from others for what you write, but you should also realize that critical revision of your writing can only strengthen your argument. Incorporating the constructive criticisms of others gives you an additional chance to "get it right." Keep in mind that editorial remarks are directed at your paper, not at you.

Third, developing the editorial skills necessary to critique the work of others will help you identify problems in your own writing. Students and professors who are perceptive editors of the writing of others can usually identify the weaknesses of their own writing and know how to revise it. That is, they can objectify their own writing, as well as the writing of others.

When others read a paper you have written, they can assess your argument only in terms of what appears before them. They cannot be expected to know the unstated information and under-standings—the thinking, outlining, research, writing, and rewrit-ing—that preceded this draft of your paper. As authors we know all of that, and consequently we may mistakenly assume our read-ers do too. Learning to distance yourself from your writing is an important first step in acquiring the skills of self-editing. I discuss how to accomplish this later in this chapter, but first let's turn to an example of how revision can create insights as well as sharpen existing ideas.

WRITING, EDITING, AND RETHINKING: AN EXAMPLE

The best way to discover how editing and rewriting can im-prove your writing is to trace their effects through a series of drafts. To illustrate this process, I have chosen a paragraph embedded in a much longer text (a Ph.D. dissertation) that, after several revisions, was incorporated into a journal-length article. (In attempting to follow my advice regarding editorial openness, I present an exam-ple from my own writing.) A single isolated paragraph, of course, cannot reveal how material from disparate sections of the original text were eventually reorganized to form the smaller article; nev-ertheless, it does show you how one, largely descriptive paragraph can form the basis of a sociological analysis.

Here is the first draft of the paragraph:

Draft I (Original)

Learning to talk "like an Alaskan" is an important part of becoming an Alaskan. It is one's claim to membership, a part of the frontier experience. Noticeably, residents of An-chorage do not refer to themselves as "Anchoragites" but as "Alaskans." Identification with the state rather than the city is strong, an obvious point to those who have seen the sprawl of urban Anchorage. Thus, the majority of the words unique to Alaska are descriptive of the region, rather than the city itself. Examples include: Outside; Cheechako;

Sourdough; cabin fever. Most others have something to do with the weather. Placing bets on the dates of "freeze up" and "break up" are annual events, as is speculation over when the "termination dust" (first snow of the season) will arrive. "White out" is not something a secretary uses but is a hazardous condition caused by "ice fog" in which light reflects off the snow yet casts no shadow. A "cache" used to be a place where food was stored out of the reach of wild animals; today it refers to a business and is often preceded by the appropriate product name, as in The Book Cache, The Stamp and Coin Cache. Though many of the cruder elements of early Alaska have vanished from the streets of downtown Anchorage, the region's frontier history lives on in daily conversation.

You probably had to restrain your impulse to edit this paragraph as soon as you began to read it. After rereading it several times, I decided that the paragraph was weak in at least three ways. First, it is plagued with imprecise language. Take, for example, the first sentence: "Learning to talk 'like an Alaskan' is an important part of becoming an Alaskan." What does it mean to describe something as "an important part"? (Do "unimportant" issues have a place in our writing?) What if I instead wrote: "Learning to talk 'like an Alaskan' is *the first step* in becoming an Alaskan"? The revised sentence leads the reader to anticipate a discussion of further stages in the process of achieving a new identity, thus lending a temporal element to the writing.

Second, as it stands, this paragraph assumes my readers have a good deal of background information about my topic. By failing to define "Outside," "Cheechako," "Sourdough," and "cabin fever" I weaken my claim that contemporary Alaskan dialogue is grounded in the imagery of its frontier history.

Third, I seem to be trying to cram too much material into one paragraph. Rereading with an eye toward revision, I decided the original paragraph could be meaningfully divided into two, because many of the examples at the end of the passage deal with the importance of climate to early Alaskan life; these examples describe things, not people. The first part of the original paragraph, by contrast, focuses on how Alaskans use a frontier vocabulary to distinguish themselves from others.

In dividing the material in the original draft into two paragraphs, I was making an *analytic* judgment. Analysis involves breaking down something into parts or categories in attempting to understand what that something is. In this example, I am trying to show the significance of a particular regional vocabulary as it is used to describe two groups: people and things.

Making these changes, I felt, took several steps in improving this passage. My revision of the original paragraph read as follows (changes from the first draft are underlined):

Draft II

Learning to talk "like an Alaskan" is the first step in becoming an Alaskan. It is one's claim to membership, an integral part of the frontier experience. Noticeably, residents of Anchorage do not refer to themselves as "Anchoragites" but as "Alaskans." Identification with the state rather than the city is strong for reasons obvious to those who have seen the urban sprawl of Anchorage. Thus, the majority of the words unique to Alaska are descriptive of the region, rather than the city itself. Most frequently heard is the term "Outside," which refers to any place which is not Alaska. Newcomers are called "Cheechakos" and old-timers "Sourdoughs," both linguistic vestiges from the days of the Alaska gold rush. The former is a derivative of "Chicago" and connotes the inexperience often displayed by newcomers to Alaska. A Sourdough, on the other hand, was a veteran prospector, the name coming from the type of bread carried on the trail.

Several other such characterizations have their origin in earlier times when climate played a major role in affecting the course of Alaskan life. The restless, claustrophobic feeling which accompanies the long hours of winter darkness is familiarly known as "cabin fever." Placing bets on the dates of "freeze up" and "break up" are annual events, as is speculation over when the "termination dust" (first snow of the season) will arrive. "White out" is not an office supply but a hazardous condition caused by "ice fog" in which light reflects off the snow casting no shadow. A "cache" used to be a place where food was stored out of the

reach of wild animals; today it usually refers to a business
and is often preceded by the appropriate product name—
hence, The Book Cache, The Stamp and Coin Cache. Though many
of the cruder elements of early Alaska have vanished from
the streets of downtown Anchorage, a part of its history
lives on in daily conversation.

Thinking that the paper was ready for an outsider reader, I
asked one of my colleagues to edit it. When she returned the paper
a few days later, she asked me what the point of it was. Somewhat
surprised, I replied that these paragraphs concerned how a
nineteenth-century frontier vocabulary could be refashioned to describe a twentieth-century experience. Wasn't that obvious from
what I had written?

After a lengthy discussion with my friend, it became clear
that I hadn't seriously asked myself *what* the theme of these paragraphs was. As I reread what I had written, I began to consider
what these many examples from Alaska said about more general
questions of language and its role in attaching people to communities. Instead of concentrating on Alaska, I began to ask "How
does this example relate to our understanding of basic social processes?" The first two sentences of the original draft hinted at the
relationship between language and community membership, but
this idea remained undeveloped, even after my revision.

In short, the problem with the second draft was that it provided a lot of evidence but failed to make a general point. The
paragraphs were primarily descriptive lists of colorful Alaskan
words and phrases. Were all of these examples alike? Did my
method of analysis need to be changed—that is, could I organize
these examples thematically, in a more meaningful way? In working through such questions, I was forced to confront the weaknesses of my previous analytic strategies. My revisions were now
leading me toward a deeper understanding of the issues embodied
in these specific illustrations gathered from my fieldwork in
Alaska.

Rethinking and revising the second draft resulted in expand-
ing the previous two paragraphs into six. Presented here is the third
draft in a slightly abbreviated version (as before, the revised text is
underlined):

Draft III

One of the fundamental institutions which facilitates group identification is language. In acquiring the language of the group, new arrivals not only come to view themselves as group members, but they also become participants in the "symbolic environment" of the group (Shibutani, 1961:490). Adoption of a common dialect, then, implies identification with the group's history and a shared perception of the group's location in social and cultural space. As Mills (1939:677) writes:

> Along with language, we acquire a set of social norms and values. A vocabulary is not merely a string of words; immanent within it are societal textures—institutional and political coordinates. Back of every vocabulary lie sets of collective action.

Residents of Anchorage, like those living in other regions of the country, employ a vernacular unique to their surroundings, and learning to "talk like an Alaskan" is the first step in becoming an Alaskan. The evaluative statements implicit in the regional vocabulary of Anchorage residents express three themes: a distinction between those living in Alaska and those living in other areas of the country; a distinction among groups of state residents; and an identification with the state as a whole, rather than with Anchorage itself—a distinction which emphasizes the more primitive side of Alaskan life.

One of the first things newcomers to Alaska notice is that virtually all Alaskans refer to non-residents as "Outsiders" and to any place which is not Alaska as "Outside." These labels which boast connotations of state chauvinism form a part of everyday conversation and act as continual reminders that others know very little about Alaska and its ways. Comments like "Outsiders have no way of knowing what we're like" are not infrequently voiced, as local residents are quick to stress the importance of having lived in the state as a necessary precondition to forming options about Alaskans.

In a similar manner language becomes a vehicle for marking differences between those who merely reside in the state and those who are "real Alaskans." The former are called "Cheechakos" and the latter "Sourdoughs," both linguistic vestiges from the days of the Alaskan gold rush. "Cheechako" is a derivative of "Chicago" and refers to the inexperience displayed by newcomers to Alaska. A Sour-dough, on the other hand, was a veteran prospector, the name coming from the bread carried on the trail. Because these two terms connote achieved status differences, the words of old-timers are sometimes used to legitimate the claims of individuals or organizations. . . .

Significantly, local residents do not refer to them-selves as "Anchoragites" for reasons obvious to those who have seen the urban sprawl of Alaska's largest city. A city of 200,000, Anchorage has been alternately portrayed as the "American nightmare" by Norman Mailer and as an "instant Albuquerque" by John McPhee. Yet despite the presence of glass office buildings, paved streets and residential sub-urbs, the livelier aspects of Alaska's past live on in the daily conversations of Anchorage residents.

Many of these characterizations have their origin in times when climate played a major role in affecting the course of Alaskan life. The restless, claustrophobic feel-ing which accompanies the long hours of winter darkness is familiarly known as "cabin fever". . . . (Cuba, 1984: 222–223)

This third draft, while preserving much of the description found in the original paragraph, is now focused analytically. The general significance of this example is explained in a new opening paragraph. References to well-known sociologists have been add-ed, establishing a link between the Alaskan example and concepts familiar to a larger professional audience. The language used to express these ideas is also somewhat formal, reflecting my percep-tion of who would be likely to read this article.

The second paragraph begins with a revised version of the first sentence of the previous draft, but is followed by a rather long sentence outlining the organization of the later paragraphs. This organizing scheme is a critical aspect of this draft. It does more than alert the reader to what follows; it provides a thematic guide sorely lacking in the first two versions. The examples that appear in the first draft as a long list of descriptive items are now grouped ac-cording to what they reveal about Alaskan life. A few more illus-trations have been included, but, for the most part, the remaining paragraphs consist of material reorganized from the earlier drafts. Although it may seem like just a matter of moving sentences from here to there, developing this framework carries the previous drafts beyond description to analysis.

This illustration from my writing demonstrates, I hope, the benefits of rewriting as rethinking. My description of the process as it appears here, however, is not entirely accurate. Presenting this example in a neat "one-two-three" draft format misrepresents the practice of writing. Writing, editing, and rethinking do not form such an orderly enterprise. Changes occur incrementally, new ideas emerge in varied sequence, and few if any of the changes shown here were the product of inspiration (or, as Paul Lazersfeld put it, an "aha experience").

It is similarly misleading to suggest that only two drafts preceded the third draft shown here. I cannot remember exactly how many times I reworked these paragraphs, but I would estimate that I made seven or eight revisions between Draft I and Draft III. That Draft III became the "final" draft had more to do with a publication deadline than with the confidence that I had at last gotten it right. All kinds of deadlines—for class projects, for committee reports, for symposium papers—bring closure to our writing. It is our responsibility as writers to allow enough time so that our first is never our final draft.

SOME HINTS ON GETTING STARTED

There is no simple formula for arriving at a writing strategy that yields consistently good results for everyone. There are, nevertheless, some general guidelines you can follow on the way to developing a habit of writing that works best for you.

1. *Describe and assess your current writing habits.* Before you can improve your writing, you must know how you write. Assume the perspective of a social scientist interested in the rituals of writing (Becker, 1986), and begin by taking an inventory of your present writing habits. When do you first begin to write an assigned paper or exam? What time of day do you usually write? What kinds of equipment (typewriters, word processors, pen) do you use? How many drafts of a paper do you normally complete

before turning it in? Where do you write? Do you write in short segments or for long periods at a time? Do you let others read your paper before you complete a last draft? Do you make notes or an outline before you begin to write? How do you assemble material that you will use in your paper? Aim for as complete a description of your writing—the whens, wheres, and hows—as possible and make notes of your observations.

Next, turn your attention to analyzing these data. Think about which habits produce the best results and which ones create problems: Do your writing habits assume a constant pattern or do they vary by course, topic, and type of writing? Do some practices consistently lead to trouble, such as failing to meet scheduled deadlines, inability to identify grammatical mistakes, or poor organization? If you take this exercise seriously, you not only will have a better idea of how to improve your writing, but will also have taken a major step toward demystifying the process of writing.

2. *Start early.* Revisions take a lot of time, and yet they are indispensable if you are going to use the process of writing as a tool for analyzing social life. Once you incorporate revising into your definition of writing an examination, oral presentation, book review, or research paper, and once you see its results, you will find that allowing time for revising is no less important than logging hours in the library preparing to write. As soon as a project is assigned, begin thinking about how you will approach it. What will be your general topic? What kinds of information could you gather to discuss this topic? Talk about your ideas with your instructor, other people in your class, or your friends. Most important, jot down notes on your ideas throughout. Making rough outlines of your topic provides a foundation for writing later on, and it also gets you into the practice of objectifying (and therefore clarifying) your thoughts. It does not matter if you write in a journal or on slips of paper that you store in a shoebox, but keep your notes, observations, and other research materials in one place. When you sit down to write a draft of your project, you will not be starting cold. Rather, you will find, to your pleasant surprise, that you have been writing all along.

3. *Read with a critical eye.* Every week we read many different kinds of writing—newspapers, magazines, novels, textbooks. Some we read for pleasure, some because they are required. We

skim some and plod through others, but, in general, we think of reading in terms of what substantive information it offers us: a review of a movie we may want to see, an interesting point to pursue in a research paper, a detailed analysis of some public issue. If we find what we read useful or interesting, it is usually because it contains what were looking for. In short, it fulfills our expectations about *content*.

In contrast, we sometimes find that our interest in what we are reading stems from how it is written. A clever organizing scheme, an unusual choice of words, or an illuminating analogy can appeal to us regardless of content. In these instances we are admiring someone's prowess as a writer. As you read, make it a point to pay close attention to what you like and what you dislike about an author's presentation. Then, try to come up with a reason for *why* you liked or disliked it. In doing so, you will have the opportunity to learn how others deal with issues of audience, tone, and argumentation and to see if analogous solutions can be incorporated into your writing. You will also be on your way to becoming a critical editor.

4. *Develop your editorial skills.* To reap the benefits of rethinking and rewriting, you must become a good editor. But how do you acquire these skills? Acquiring useful editorial skills takes practice, and there is no single best way to edit a piece of writing. Some people prefer to edit papers line by line, checking each sentence for clarity, conciseness, and grammar. Others prefer to focus on questions of organization, balance, and style as they affect the general shape and content of a paper. Obviously, some combination of these editorial styles will yield the best results. You can find some suggestions concerning both specific and general revisions of drafts in Chapter 8.

Bear in mind that writing is a collegial enterprise. Social scientists, like all academicians, read and comment on each other's writing. You may have noticed that authors of books and articles you have encountered in your research usually acknowledge the assistance of others. Some of the editorial insights that emerge in a piece of writing are the author's; some come from other readers; and some—often the most helpful—result from the author's discussion with his or her colleagues. Enlisting the aid of a circle of editorial friends can improve your writing immeasurably. Just remember to return the favor of exchanging papers and to give appropriate credit for editorial suggestions that you adopt.*

If you receive an edited copy of your work from someone else, ask your editor for specific information about your paper's major weaknesses. Don't feel that you have to accept all of the comments of your editor. Your disagreement with an editor may, in fact, spawn a productive debate about your writing that leads to rethinking and revision in another direction. The primary purpose of editing is to open up a dialogue, not simply to acquiesce to the suggestions of others.

If you are editing your own work—and all writers must develop the habit of editing their own work—you need to develop ways to distance yourself from your writing. One simple step in that direction involves transferring your writing from one medium to another. Readers, as well as authors, respond quite differently to typewritten, prepublication drafts and printed, published copies of the same material. If you usually draft papers in longhand, try typing them before editing. If your first drafts arise out of interactions with a word processor, make your revisions on a printed copy. "Transcribing" your writing in this manner provides an alternative context for your words that is essential in objectifying your thoughts. Of course, allowing ample time between writing and editing also helps in this process. That is why it is impossible to overstate the need to start writing early.

---

*Students are often reluctant to discuss class assignments with their friends or to ask them to read papers they have written, fearing that such practices violate codes of academic honor. Although independent effort is expected on individual projects, most professors welcome student editing groups in their classes. If you are worried about your professors' opinions about student editing, discuss this option with them. And if you discuss your assignment with other students, include a proper acknowledgment in a footnote or preface to your paper.

2

Summaries and Reviews of Social Science Literature

This chapter examines several kinds of writing that are based on what other social scientists have discovered. Abstracts, annotations, book reviews, and literature reviews form a hierarchy that moves from summarizing social science research to analyzing and criticizing it. Abstracts and annotations are summaries of social science research that stand on their own as finished pieces of social science writing. Book reviews begin with summaries, and the analysis that book reviewing entails figures heavily into a survey of a body of research. A review of the literature, in turn, is the foundation for a research paper in which you analyze data you have collected yourself. How to organize a research paper based on original data is the topic of the next chapter.

ABSTRACTS, ANNOTATIONS, AND OTHER SUMMARIES

Summaries of social science research appear in a number of forms. *Abstracts* found at the beginning of papers, articles, and books outline the essential elements of the work. On the basis of the abstract alone, a social science researcher often decides whether or not to read the abstracted article or book. *Annotations* of other people's research may appear in bibliographies, giving the reader brief information beyond that appearing in the title. And at a more informal level—for example, as you prepare for an examination or class paper—you usually want to summarize course materials to avoid the need to return to original sources each time you want to recall the main point of a book or article.

Whether you are preparing a summary for yourself or for others, it will be useful only if it translates, as faithfully as possible, many words into few. More than any other form of social science writing, writing abstracts and other summaries requires concise language and precise usage. Most professional journals specify strict length requirements for abstracts (250 words; one or two paragraphs), and annotations are usually much shorter (five sentences or fewer). You have more latitude in preparing summaries for your own use, but you will usually find that their usefulness diminishes as their size increases. Underlining every sentence in an article seldom improves your understanding of social life or saves you time.

Don't fall into the trap of assuming that summaries are easy-to-write, mindless exercises. To write an effective abstract or annotation, you must be able to read for the main ideas in a piece of research, recognize the relevance of these ideas for a particular audience, and organize them clearly and concisely. Although there is no rigid format for preparing summaries, you may find it useful to ask these questions of each work:

1. *What question is posed by this work?* This central question should guide your reading of all social science literature. In a research report or journal article, this question is probably phrased in terms of some hypothesis or set of hypotheses outlining the relationships among a set of variables. For instance, "Educational attainment is affected by initial work values; it also has socializing effects on work values and affects occupational selection" (Lindsay and Knox, 1984). In a longer piece the thesis may be stated less formally (e.g., "The debate over the role of heredity in aggressive behavior continues to rage.") As a principal goal of your writing is economy of language, try to express the main ideas of a book or article using a vocabulary familiar to those working within a specific field. Thus, if you are investigating the effects of government

regulation on the airline industry, you might want to phrase the thesis in terms of *organizational environments,* a concept that is well grounded in the sociological literature on organizations. Doing so not only places the research in a larger theoretical context, but it also makes it easier for you to compare it with other studies that address the same general question.

2. *What is the method of data collection and analysis?* Readers will want to know how the major research question was investigated. Was an interview administered? Were field observations made? Were previous studies reanalyzed or were new data collected? Was the research analyzed qualitatively (nonnumerically) or quantitatively (numerically)? When and where was the research conducted? Answers to these questions place the work within broad categories of social science research and expedite comparisons among several pieces of research.

3. *What are the findings?* Given the hypotheses to be tested, what did the researchers discover? It may be difficult to state succinctly the findings of the work you are summarizing, particularly if it is a book. Identifying the specific thesis of a book helps, because the findings should address this thesis directly. Note any explicit qualifications of the results of the research, such as limitations to generalizing the results to a larger population, or the possibility that variables not measured may distort the findings.

As you begin to write the summary, don't hesitate to follow the organization of the work being summarized. For example, the chapter headings of a book or the standard format of research writing (introduction, methods, results, analysis) may provide a framework for your summary. This works well if the author's argument is organized logically and presented clearly. If not, you will want to create your own outline for organizing the summary. I suggest, however, placing the thesis in the first sentence of the summary regardless of how the work itself is organized.

Keep in mind that a summary does *not* include comments on or analysis of the material being summarized. It objectively—and briefly—reports what the original material offers. You might begin your summary by identifying the author of the material, but don't introduce each sentence with something like "Smith says. . . ." It will be obvious to the reader that Smith is the author of the material being summarized. Also, quotation marks are usually not needed, as it is assumed that the summary is reporting the source directly.

Examples

An abstract from an article appearing in a professional journal, an entry from an annotated bibliography, and a summary of a book by a student for a course are shown in the following examples. Note the different style of each summary.

AN ABSTRACT

The Resurgence of Sharecropping: Historical Anomaly or Political Strategy?

Although traditional economic theories regard sharecropping as inefficient and likely to dwindle in systems of capitalist commodity production, sharecropping has exhibited remarkable persistence under a range of historical conditions. This article explores the reasons for the unexpected tenacity of share farming and considers its implications for the analysis of rural class structure and agrarian change. Using the example of the resurgence of sharecropping in the California strawberry industry, the paper demonstrates that political constraints on agricultural production are key determinants of the contemporary adoption of sharecropping, establishing a context in which sharecropping not only facilitates but is recreated by capitalist accumulation. (Wells, 1984:1)

AN ANNOTATION

Epstein, Richard A. *Takings: Private Property and the Power of Eminent Domain*. Cambridge, Mass.: Harvard University Press, 1985. Pp. xi + 362.

In this analysis of the eminent domain clause of the Constitution, Epstein argues that in contrast to other guarantees in the Bill of Rights, the takings clause has been interpreted quite narrowly. He contends that our system of private property and limited government is not elastic enough to accommodate the massive reforms of the New Deal, that the redistribution of wealth is not a proper role of government, and that the constitutionality of such practices as zoning, rent control, and workers' compensation is questionable. (American Bar Foundation, 1986:972)

A STUDENT SUMMARY

Perkins, H. Wesley. 1985. "Religious Traditions, Parents and Peers as Determinants of Alcohol and Drug Use Among College Students." Review of Religious Research 27:15–31.

Perkins found that alcohol consumption differed among students according to their religious backgrounds: Catholics consumed the most alcohol, Jews the least, and Protestants fell in between the two. The differences in alcohol consumption (as measured by mean scores) are statistically significant ($p<0.05$) for first- and second-year students but are not significant for upperclass students. Thus, although alcohol consumption among first- and second-year Jewish students was significantly less compared to their Catholic and Protestant peers, upperclass students drank at roughly the same rate, regardless of their religious affiliation. This study suggests that college may have a liberal effect on drinking among Jewish students which is not present for either Catholic or Protestant students.

BOOK REVIEWS

Unlike summaries, book reviews often reveal clearly what a writer thinks about a particular work, that is, they include *evaluation*. In moving beyond a succinct restatement of a book's or article's main points, they provide a forum for the reviewer's voice, and, at the same time, serve an important research function for social scientists. Book reviews are usually written fairly soon after a book is published, allowing scholars to keep abreast of new developments in their field. Because they are brief (usually between 600 and 1000 words), book reviews provide a valuable guide to those conducting library research. Book reviews do not simply lavish praise on some authors and hurl criticism at others; they provide a cogent summary of a work, point out both its good and bad qualities, and often place it within an established literature.

As with all types of social science writing, a book review is written for a specific audience. Knowing who will most likely read what we have written influences what we write. Some journals, such as *Contemporary Sociology,* are devoted exclusively to reviews. Written and read by specialists in many subfields of sociology, the reviews in such journals assume the readers have a good deal of background information. Other reviews, for instance those appearing in newspapers or magazines, may make few assumptions about what potential readers know. They may, for example, have to identify a writer who is known to everyone within the profession but unknown to the general public. Because reviews for the general public can take little for granted, they may contain more summary or exposition than analysis.

Of course, just as the audience dictates what information will be included in a book review, the author's background is equally constraining. If you are not an expert in the field of family sociology, for example, you may find it difficult to write a scholarly critique of Lillian Rubin's *Worlds of Pain*. This does not mean that you couldn't find something interesting to say about her book, just that you would probably write a review different from one by someone who teaches family sociology. You might construct an argument challenging (or supporting) the logic of Rubin's analysis, while the instructor might dwell more on the contribution of her work to the literature on family studies.

There is no formula for writing a good book review, but some guidelines can provide a foundation for review writing. First, don't try to cover everything in the book. True, you will want to give the reader an idea of the entire book—perhaps in a one-paragraph summary—but you can then go on to focus on its chief strengths or weaknesses, or both. Organize the review around the thesis of the book (and its subthesis, if relevant); avoid using the table of contents as your organizing key.

Second, support your arguments with evidence from the book. Use examples that provide the best illustrations of the points you make, trying to phrase them in your own words while retaining their contextual meaning. Reserve the use of direct quotations for those times when they are essential to making your point. If, for example, a book is especially well written (or badly written), and you are going to comment on its style, fairness requires that you include a sample quotation or two. If you do include quotations, make them brief and include proper citations to the book. (See the section on citation format in Chapter 7.)

Third, if you are reviewing a book in an area in which you have some familiarity, avoid using the review as an opportunity to display your own competence. Remember, readers of your review are interested in the competence of the author whose work you are reviewing, not your own. Follow closely the advice of John Updike: "Do not imagine yourself a caretaker of any tradition, an enforcer of any party standards, a warrior in any ideological battle, a corrections officer of any kind. Review the book, not the reputation."

As a related caution, don't criticize authors because they fail to write the book you think they should have written. Identify an author's intentions and judge the merits of the book based on those intentions. Valid criticisms may be lodged against deceptive advertising, but guard against asking too much of the author. If a book purports to be an institutional analysis of educational reform, do not expect it to address the social-psychological effects of curricular changes on students and teachers.

How do you go about organizing a book review? In the following, I have modified slightly a set of guidelines Barnet and Stubbs (1986) offer as a general organizing scheme for a short review, say 500 to 1000 words:

1. An introductory paragraph identifying the work and its author, presenting the thesis of the book, and giving some indication of whether the author achieves the stated purpose of the book.

2. A paragraph or two summarizing the book and relating it (where possible) to other books in this field. (This might be a slightly elaborated version of a summary of the book as described in the preceding section.)

3. A paragraph noting the strengths of the book (if any).

4. A paragraph noting the weaknesses of the book (if any).

5. A concluding paragraph that conveys, on balance, your assessment of the strengths and weaknesses of the book. (Does the book succeed?)

A variation on this form of social science writing is the *review essay*. Review essays are critical reviews of a book or set of books written by experts in a particular field of study. They are longer than the typical review and devote more time to an assessment of the work within an established research tradition. (Often they include citations to related works.) Review essays, more than regular reviews, provide a forum for the reviewer to engage in a dialogue with the author, and, consequently, lean more toward analysis than description.

Examples

Reprinted here are two reviews of David Rothman's *The Discovery of the Asylum.* The first was written by a college student for a required course in writing; the second was written by an historian and appeared in a professional journal. The differences in qualifications of the reviewers and the audiences to whom they are writing should be clear as you compare these reviews.

A STUDENT REVIEW

Elizabeth Stone
Writing 125S

An Examination of Asylums

The Discovery of the Asylum by David Rothman is a thought-provoking analysis of the origin and evolution of American institutions. Rothman describes the tumultuous events and public opinion that shaped the way deviants were treated during the eighteenth and nineteenth centuries. Using the perspective of social history, he examines the problems that developed from the decision to isolate society's misfits in asylums.

The book begins with a discussion of the treatment of deviants from the Colonial period through the Civil War. The colonists believed that deviance was the result of individual weaknesses instead of a flaw in community structure. Workhouses and almshouses were intended to discourage vagrants from invading communities and to house the poor who would "monetarily inconvenience" other residents. But in response to philosophical and practical changes—an emphasis on reason and a growing population—these practices shifted to a desire to "cure" deviants. Now, people began to search for the roots of deviance within society itself. The cure for improper behavior would be found through a system of rational codes.

It was out of this climate that the institution was born, complete with humanitarian and reformatory goals. The penitentiary, the almshouse, and the asylum were run on the principles of order, discipline, and routine. Rothman describes how ideas for the reform and rehabilitation of deviants were lost and never recovered in the blind concern for the institution's physical organization and structure. For example, in the prison system, convict labor, lack of parole, and prison crowding eventually turned the asylum into a custodial institution. "The promise of reform had built up the asylums; the functionalism of custody perpetuated them" (240).

This historical account is appealing, largely because of Rothman's style. He writes with a wry, slightly sarcastic tone, describing the ideas of the time while conveying his personal opinions. To illustrate, consider these words on corporal punishment in orphanages, a practice of which Rothman obviously did not approve: "A good dose of institutionalization could only work to the child's benefit" (209). The use of frequent quotations reinforces his historical perspective and paints a vivid picture of early American asylums. Unfortunately, Rothman fails to discuss anti-institutional movements during this time, and he offers little insight into the institutional experience from the inside. Nevertheless, Rothman's argument is well-documented. He reviews a different institution in each chapter, showing the effect of this asylum on society from its hopeful beginning to its failure.

Despite these minor shortcomings, The Discovery of the Asylum tells a fascinating story. These institutions were established not only to show the national government in a favorable light but also to provide a ready alternative for the accelerating disintegration of the Colonial order. If we accept Rothman's argument that rehabilitation was merely a secondary consideration in the development of asylums, we must confront the question: Can the goal of curing deviance be meaningfully introduced into these institutions? Rothman's conclusions give us some hope that such a thing is possible: "We need not remain trapped in inherited answers" (295).

A SCHOLARLY REVIEW

The Discovery of the Asylum: Social Order and Disorder in the New Republic by David J. Rothman. Boston, Little, Brown and Company, 1971. — xx. 376 pp. $12.50.

In a book that is simultaneously a work of history and social criticism, David J. Rothman presents an interpretation of American society during the first half of the ninetenth century that is both provocative and disturbing. His thesis, which is clear and lucid, is relatively simple. By the early nineteenth century, according to Rothman, the traditional and stable society of the colonial period had begun to disintegrate. Aware of the momentous changes that were taking place, Americans were uncertain as to how they should meet the challenges of the new order and restore the social cohesion they deemed so vital to society. Obsessed with deviant and dependent behavior, they ultimately came to the conclusion that "to comprehend and control abnormal behavior promised to be the first step in establishing a new system for stabilizing the community, for binding citizens together."

The solution that Americans adopted, writes Rothman, involved the creation of the "asylum"—an institution that would reform criminals, juvenile delinquents, poor and indigent groups, mentally ill persons, and all other deviants whose abnormal behavior might or did threaten society. The result was an incredible proliferation of prisons, almshouses, houses of refuge, and mental hospitals, to cite only a few. Although most of these institutions abandoned any pretense at rehabilitation and rapidly degenerated into custodial institutions that served as "a dumping ground for social undesirables," they survived because it was easier to incarcerate undesirables than to seek new and different solutions.

While *The Discovery of the Asylum* will undoubtedly appeal to many contemporary readers who will share its author's anti-institutionalism and moral outrage, as a work of historical scholarship it leaves something to be desired. First, it indiscriminately confuses institutions that have superficial resemblances. A mental hospital—whatever its failures and shortcomings—*did* care for sick individuals, since its patient population included substantial numbers of cases of general paresis and senile psychoses (both of which were clearly of organic origin). To identify jails, almshouses, and mental hospitals as variations of one species is inaccurate, even though they had much in common. Secondly, a comparative approach casts grave doubts over the validity of Rothman's thesis. If confinement in specialized "asylums" was the response of a nation which feared change and saw institutionalization as a means of social control, how then does one explain the fact that these very same institutions (jails, almshouses, mental hospitals) appeared in England and on the continent either earlier or at the very same time as in America. Yet there is little evidence to indicate that the social order in Europe was undergoing the same or a similar process of disintegration. Thirdly, the book is simplistic; it deals with complex social processes without the subtleties and nuances that mark sophisticated scholarship. Rothman's approach to history is too rationalistic and intellectualized, for he assumes a one-to-one relationship between intent and consequence. Finally, the evidence used is either incomplete or one-sided. The book in general is not based on manuscript sources, which would have added a dimension that is presently lacking. To write about mental hospitals and yet not to examine the extensive and rich collections of Dorothea L. Dix, Thomas S. Kirkbride, Samuel B. Woodward, Pliny Earle, Edward Jarvis, and others, is unforgivable. Morever, Rothman has conveniently summarized all of the evidence that validates his thesis, but has neglected or slighted the material that contradicts his interpretation.

I am sorry to be so critical of this book, which despite its defects has many shrewd and brilliant insights. Had Rothman not been so intent on reducing all phenomena to one simple thesis and offering a lesson to our own generation, his book could have been a major contribution to American social history. That it is not is partly a product of the confusion of ideology with scholarship.

GERALD N. GROB
Rutgers University

LITERATURE REVIEWS

Scientific research is informed by questions others have posed and answers they have received. It points to new directions by seeking answers to previously unanswered questions, by posing questions that have yet to be asked, and by challenging answers that have been commonly accepted. In short, scientific inquiries are made in response to previous research and seek to advance our understanding of social life incrementally. For that reason, social scientists—whether professors or undergraduates— want to know what others have discovered before they begin investigations of their own.

One convenient way of finding out about previous research is to locate a literature review covering the topic that interests you. Literature reviews are critical compilations of previous research that outline established findings, conflicting evidence and gaps in a body of scholarship. Like abstracts and book reviews, their quality rests heavily on their effective summary of the work of others. Literature reviews, however, demand more of their authors than do these other forms of writing. The author must not only be familiar with a large quantity of previous research, but also be able to classify the materials and critically analyze them. To put it another way, literature reviews are exercises in writing comparisons.

Because authors of literature reviews hope to make valid comparisons among a number of related studies, they are forced to pay attention to the immense variation characterizing social science research. One may find that two studies arrive at apparently contradictory conclusions only to discover that the same concept (i.e., a word or phrase that represents a class of phenomena) has been measured in different ways. In one survey of many published articles on poverty, for example, the authors found that the way in which "poverty" was measured determined the number of people considered to be living in substandard economic conditions (Williamson and Hyer, 1975). Variation in the absolute dollar amount establishing the poverty level was one obvious source of the different results, but a number of other factors also influenced the research findings: Did the authors consider individual or family income? Were data collected in a single year or over a period of years? Were forms of public subsistence included in the calculation of welfare status? This is but one example of where research investigations may share *nominal definitions* of a concept (in this example, "poverty") but rely on different *operational definitions* (ways of measuring poverty).

Making valid comparisons in a literature review requires not only close scrutiny of how concepts are measured but attention to many of the technical aspects of social research as well. Consequently, the information you gather from each study must be more detailed than that used in preparing a review of a single book. Literature reviews begin here, with the compilation of many summaries. After the results of previous research have been summarized, they must be organized and then evaluated.

Summarizing Previous Research

For each entry into the review, keep a separate outline listing each of the following:

1. *A complete bibliographic reference.* Begin each entry with a formal reference to the work being summarized. Here is one example:

> Wells, Miriam J. 1984. "The Resurgence of Sharecropping: Historical Anomaly or Political Strategy?" *American Journal of Sociology* 90 (July):1–29.

Recording this information in standard form will save time later when you are compiling a bibliography for the review. Separate pages or cards will also ease the task of alphabetizing listings. (For more on bibliographic form, see Chapter 7.)

2. *The major question(s) posed in this study.* Be specific in your description of the research hypothesis of each study. If the authors explicitly state their hypothesis, record it directly, making sure to acknowledge it as a verbatim quotation (i.e., using page number references and quotation marks). Paraphrasing and summarizing can always be done later. If your source is a book that addresses several dimensions of a widely researched concept, you may choose to focus your summary on only one or two chapters of the work. It is unlikely, for example, that you would be asked (or decide on your own) to conduct a literature review of all previous research on, say, alienation. Instead, you might wish to concentrate on the social-psychological effects of alienation in the workplace.

3. *The method of investigation.* Is the study primarily qualitative or quantitative? What mode of observation was employed (e.g., questionnaires, personal interviews, field observations, archival searches)? Also, note the time frame for the study if one is given.

4. *The major variables and their operational definitions.* As mentioned previously, the way in which concepts are defined guides the

findings as well as the implications of a piece of research. Record how each variable is measured and, where possible, identify variables as *dependent, independent,* or *control.*

Dependent variables are the focus of a research investigation; they denote sets of attributes that are thought to be caused by other, *independent variables.* In the hypothesis "Income varies directly with education," the dependent variable would be income, the independent variable education. The more education a person had, the higher we would expect his or her income to be. If a dependent variable is, in fact, affected by one or more independent variables, manipulating the independent variables should result in a change in the dependent variable. If the researchers were concerned that the effect of education on income might be influenced by whether a person was black or white, they might introduce race as a *control variable.* Generally, control variables pose the question: In the presence of Z (a control variable), does the relationship between X (an independent variable) and Y (a dependent variable) change? In this example, introducing race as a control would entail comparing the relationship between education and income for whites to the same relationship for blacks. Paying particular attention to the use of control variables is important because these variables may qualify a general research question explored in your survey of the literature.

5. *The study population.* How is the sample of observations for this study defined? Is it composed of individuals, groups, or organizations (e.g., the family, cities, or IBM), or a collection of artifacts (e.g., newspapers, television commercials, or magazine advertisements)? Was the study conducted in this country or abroad? Was a method of sample selection employed in selecting a group for study? Another source of variation in research findings is the differences that arise among study populations. An obvious example is that of attitudinal surveys concerning controversial issues that are administered to different groups. Opinions regarding the legally established age limits for buying and consuming alcohol are likely to differ depending on whether the survey is administered in a small town or a large city, at a college or a church, or to college sophomores or legislative representatives.

6. *The findings.* In describing the outcome of the research, record specific information detailing the interrelationships among the variables studied. Don't just write "Age had a significant effect

on voter participation"; instead, list the magnitude and level of the effect, for example, "Age was positively correlated with voter participation ($r = 0.37$). This correlation was statistically significant at the 0.05 level." Although this type of statistical information is likely to be provided only in quantitative studies, similar care should be taken to note the particulars of qualitative findings. For example, "Regardless of their age or race, men were more likely than women to give their unsolicited opinion about the proposed change in club membership policies."

7. *The author's conclusions.* After reporting research findings, social scientists often evaluate their own analyses. They may comment on implications of their findings for future research, note the similarity between their work and previously published work, or argue that their results are similarly descriptive of other times or places. Try to record these evaluative remarks separately from your report of the research findings, because these evaluative remarks may serve as the basis for comment in your literature review. You may find that authors who present similar findings come to different conclusions, or you may decide that you object to the interpretation an author has placed on his or her data.

8. *Your comments.* Leave a place at the end of each entry to list your response to the research. While accumulating source material, you may find yourself noting similarities or differences among studies as you read them. Making a note of this observation at the time you read the study may ease the task of organizing your summaries. You may also want to use this space to jot down any reservations you have with the author's methods or conclusions.

Organizing the Summaries

Literature reviews are usually organized in one of two ways, topically or chronologically. Most often, they are structured *topically:* previous research is divided into segments representing conceptual subsets of some larger issue. For example, a review of a concept such as alienation, which has identifiable dimensions, may logically be organized around these dimensions—for instance, powerlessness, meaninglessness, or normlessness. Similarly, reviews of a particular institution, such as the criminal courts, may be organized according to different methodologies through which they have been studied. If you are interested in judicial sentencing, for example, you may find that it makes sense to separate entries for your review into qualitative (nonnumerical) and quantitative (numerical) sections. This is especially important in cases in which different methodologies have been used to ask different questions. A qualitative approach such as making field observations in a criminal courtroom may yield valuable insights into the dynamics between defendant and judge, but such an approach is not the best way to examine the relationship between a defendant's prior record and sentencing outcomes over a twenty-year period. Investigations of the latter type are best undertaken through an archival search of court documents and lend themselves to quantitative manipulation.

The second common approach to organizing literature is *chronological*. Ordering the entries in your review according to when they were published provides an historical context for your topic. If your goal is to discuss a particular concept from its emergence to its present use within a discipline, a chronological review is a useful analytic strategy. It reveals which contributions have been the most significant (in terms of repeated references by others); it points to periods of dormancy during which few researchers were working on a particular topic; and it identifies paradigmatic shifts in a discipline as they emerge out of well-established perspectives.

It also makes good sense to organize a review chronologically if you wish to follow the development of social science research alongside historical developments occurring *outside* its boundaries. Consider, for example, the research conducted by American sociologists on racial attitudes in this country. If you were reviewing this literature, you would not be surprised to find that questions attempting to measure race relations have varied over time. In 1940, social scientists were asking respondents whether blacks should be allowed to ride on the same bus with whites; in 1975, their surveys contained questions about busing black and white school children. How the questions were worded—substituting "black" for "Negro," for example—would also differ across the materials you encounter in your research (Schuman, Steeh, and Bobo, 1985). Using a temporal framework for a review of a topic such as attitudes toward race relations can help you trace the currents of social change as they emerge and are manifested in social science research. This type of chronology often dramatically illustrates the force with which history shapes what social scientists consider worth knowing, as well as how they go about knowing it.

Preparing a Critical Response

You may have noticed from these remarks that both how summaries are prepared and how they are organized provide implicit strategies for a critical response. This means that as you get ready to write, you will probably have some sense of the major ideas that will guide your review, keeping in mind that reviews are essentially comparative exercises. In recording the same types of information for each piece of research, you will have established the basis for comparison along several lines of inquiry: purpose of the research, research methods, operationalization of major concepts, observations from different populations, discrepancies in findings, or differences in the interpretation of results. The number of comparisons you could address is probably large, but how do you go about constructing your argument?

Let's assume that you want to compare a number of studies concerned with the same hypotheses but differing in their findings. One way of proceeding is first to discuss each piece of research in turn, and then conclude by attempting to account for the discrepancies in outcome among them. This is an effective method if the number of entries into the review is small; if you are reviewing a large body of research, your audience is likely to become mired in a catalog of descriptions, waiting for your analysis. You can avoid this problem by selecting one or two studies that represent broadly supported findings, using these as emblematic of a group. For instance, you might write the following: "Robertson's (1972) analysis of crime in Atlanta showed that most thefts are never reported to the police." After describing this principal entry, you could follow it with something like "Smith (1983), McFarland (1966), and Jones (1985) report similar findings in their investigations of other American cities."

Try, also, to limit your descriptions of each study to the essential elements that will be used in the comparison. Provide enough information about the research to amass sufficient evidence for your analysis, but do not yield to the temptation to give long descriptive passages of each work. Each piece of research does not deserve equal (and brief) attention in your review. Length of treatment is one means of suggesting whether a study is major or minor. Reserve longer summaries (and critiques) for landmark studies that inspire many others.

An outline for such a literature review might be as follows:

  I. Statement of thesis
 II. Literature reviewed
     A. First study
     B. Second study
     C. Third study
III. Comparative analysis
     A. Similarities
     B. Differences
 IV. Conclusion (in which you attempt to explain points of comparison or contrast)

An alternative strategy is to begin by describing the characteristics of research shared by several studies, and then move to an analysis of their differences. This approach has the advantage of easily conforming to a topical structure because the generic aspects of the research—the findings, methods, and so forth—guide your analysis, rather than the discrete research investigations themselves.

A corresponding outline might look like this:

  I. Statement of thesis
 II. Similarities in the research
     A. First similarity
     B. Second similarity
     C. Third similarity
III. Differences in the research
     A. First difference
     B. Second difference
     C. Third difference
 IV. Conclusion (in which you reconcile similarities and differences)

Whatever type of comparative analysis you adopt, you must guide your readers through the review by beginning with a strong thesis statement. Let them know exactly how the review is organized and what your analytic strategy will be. If appropriate, specify the historical period covered in your review. Doing so at the outset may deflect later criticism that you have failed to exhaust the literature on your topic.

Here is the introduction to a review of the literature on sex roles:

> Hundreds of studies have addressed sex-role differentiation, but the findings have not been systematically integrated to form a cumulative body of knowledge. Our understanding of the processes by which sex roles influence the system of social stratification is especially limited. We add our review to those of others (e.g., Lipman-Blumen and Tickamyer, 1975; Pleck, 1977; Waite and Hudis, 1980; Scanzoni and Fox, 1980) in order to further this synthesis, identifying critical theoretical questions and effective research strategies.
>
> In this paper we examine recent literature on the sexual division of labor. We are particularly concerned with sex roles as fundamental channeling and integrative mechanisms. The review focuses on two major areas: the division of labor in the family and in the economy. Although they are obviously interrelated, we first address sexual differentiation in each realm separately before considering sex roles as an integrating mechanism coordinating work and family roles. (Miller and Garrison, 1982:237)

Extend your introductory remarks by using signposts to guide your audience through the body of your review. Use short section titles or strong transitional sentences to signify moving from one study or issue to another. If the review is long, provide intermediate summaries of subsections of the review. Some readers may be interested in only one or two topics covered in the review; intermediate summaries may prove helpful to their research.

As you conclude your review, make sure you go beyond a simple summary statement. Don't be afraid to give your own interpretation of this body of research. Now that you have reflected on the similarities and differences in these studies, which questions have been addressed and which have been left unanswered? What kinds of work appear more valuable in retrospect? What is the next logical step in this chain of cumulative research? What contributions might interdisciplinary work make to the research in this field? Remember that a good literature review not only reveals what social scientists have done; it also serves as the foundation for future work within an established discipline.

3

Papers Based on Original Research

Research papers are the most frequently assigned type of writing in intermediate and upper-level courses in the social sciences. They require an ability to do several kinds of writing well. To write a good research paper, you must be able to summarize previous research (as you would in book reviewing), critically evaluate and compare several related studies (as you would in a literature review), and, in the end, briefly summarize a lengthy paper composed of your findings (as you would in abstracting a journal article).

Research papers can be roughly divided into two categories. The first category of research papers (often called *term papers*) relies heavily on the work of others in constructing and supporting a thesis. In this type of writing, your primary task is to organize and critically evaluate previous research on your chosen topic. The second category of papers, by contrast, describes and analyzes observations resulting from original research. Here your principal focus is on the data you have collected; research appearing in scholarly publications is used to set the context for or supplement your own observations, but a paper of this sort chiefly presents and analyzes new data. This chapter focuses on writing papers based on original research, that is, papers of the second type; term papers involving library research are discussed in the following chapter.

QUANTITATIVE VERSUS QUALITATIVE RESEARCH

Social scientists make a broad distinction between two methodologies used to collect data—quantitative methodologies and qualitative methodologies. *Quantitative methodologies* are appropriate when the goal of the study is to represent some phenomenon numerically. We often associate these methods with survey research in which questionnaires—say, on smoking habits or attitudes toward drunk driving—are completed by respondents or surveys are administered and the results tallied. But quantitative methods are also employed in many other types of research: studies of community crime rates, aggregate shifts in population (how many people moved, when and where), or language and communication (how many times sexist pronouns appeared in a series of children's books), to name but a few. The results of quantitative studies often assume the form of statistics (i.e., summary measures describing sample outcomes). On the basis of these statistics, researchers may attempt to make inferences about a larger population from which their sample is drawn.

Qualitative methodologies, on the other hand, are best suited to answering questions about social organization and social processes. For example, how does one "become" a marijuana user (Becker, 1963), learn to identify and respond to strangers (Lofland, 1973; Suttles, 1968), or deal with mental illness in the context of family life (Yarrow et al., 1972)? Field research, in which social scientists describe and analyze the nuances of social life as they occur in some setting, is a qualitative approach frequently used by anthropologists, sociologists, and other social scientists. Qualitative researchers may, of course, report numerical findings to bolster their arguments, but they are chiefly concerned with illustrating in rich detail social interaction as it occurs in limited settings. In doing so, they develop typologies or modal categories of social action (e.g., different leadership styles) and point to the limitations of these categories as revealed in the variation among the persons they study.

Philosophical and methodological differences separate quantitative and qualitative research, but both kinds of research papers use basically the same format. For that reason, I discuss both types of research papers together. The major difference between qualitative and quantitative writing appears in the presentation of research findings, and it is at that point I will pause to call attention to some of their differences.

ORGANIZING THE PAPER

The most common format for organizing a paper reporting original research follows the model of hypothesis testing. This model involves the interplay between inductive reasoning, in which the social scientist tries to construct general principles from a set of observations, and deductive reasoning, in which general principles are used to explain a set of observations. Hypothesis testing is the bridge between the "real world" and social theory. A trained social scientist working within this framework always sees the world in terms of the question: What is this an example of?

This doesn't mean that social scientists don't get caught up in the fascinating details of everyday life. They do. They may wonder why some members of their local school committee hold the opinions they do, why some women in their neighborhood enjoy being homemakers and some do not, and why some relatives are delighted with their life in a retirement community in Florida while others are sorry they have left their old homes in Michigan. But as social scientists writing for other social scientists, they must search for a way of explaining the immense variation of social life in terms of some broader, unifying theme. School committee voting records become data for a study of community politics, interviews with homemakers inform a study of the multiple roles available to women, and opinions about moving to Florida shed light on attitudes toward elderly migration. Although few social scientists may be interested in the contextual details of a specific research project, many may be eager to hear an investigator's general interpretation of these data.

The importance of framing specific empirical observations (e.g., Mrs. Brooks plays bridge twice a week and regularly volunteers in a local hospital) in terms of some larger question (e.g., How do retired people spend their time?) carries over to how social scientists report the results of their research. Research reports appearing in scholarly journals are fairly consistent in style and tone. They tend to be formal in that most do not use first-person pronouns. ("This study explores the relationship between academic performance and career choices," rather than "I will study . . ."). This practice, however, has recently declined, and one now sometimes reads: "In this study I explore the relationship between academic performance and career choices." Journal articles seldom contain contractions ("Women cannot . . .," rather than "Women can't . . .") or colloquial expressions ("adolescents" rather than "teenagers").

Although not always lively, journal articles tend to be highly informative. Most important, they usually follow a standard format. Research papers normally comprise these parts, with some latitude in their ordering:

1. Title page
2. Abstract (if appropriate)
3. Introduction/statement of problem
4. Research methods
5. Findings/results
6. Discussion/conclusions
7. Notes (if appropriate)
8. References
9. Appendixes (if appropriate)

A research paper should always include part 1, parts 3 through 6, and part 8. The other parts—abstracts, notes, and appendixes—are optional; their inclusion depends on the length of the paper, your specific needs in writing the paper, and your audience. For example, you may not need to write an abstract for a short (five- to seven-page) research paper assigned in an intermediate sociology class. But published research reports are almost all abstracted, regardless of their length.

The parts of the research paper are discussed in the order presented here, even though you probably will not write them in this order. It is unlikely, for example, that you will be able to select an appropriate title or write a good abstract before you have written the body of your paper.

THE TITLE

Good titles are difficult to construct. They tax your skills at summarizing because here, more than in any sentence you may write, every word counts. Everyone wants to begin his or her paper with a catchy title, one that will stick in a reader's head, but if you choose this route, make sure your title accurately conveys the thesis of your paper. One way to blend interest with substance is to follow a general title with a more informative subtitle. Less frequently used in journal-type writing, this pattern is frequently employed in book titles. Here are some book titles that strike me as especially memorable:

Wayward Puritans: A Study in the Sociology of Deviance

Stigma: Notes on the Management of Spoiled Identity

The Urban Villagers: Group and Class in the Life of Italian-Americans

To Dwell Among Friends: Personal Networks in Town and City

Above all, titles should be informative. They should give enough information to convey the general, theoretical focus of the paper as well as the specific variables that are used in the research. Try to do all this, but in the fewest words possible. Titles usually do not describe the exact setting of the research (e.g., Wellesley College, New York City, or General Motors).

1. POOR: An Analysis of Neighborhood Surveys
   IMPROVED: Attitudes toward Racial Integration in an Urban Neighborhood

2. POOR: Staying Home
   IMPROVED: Staying Home: Suburban Homemakers Look at Themselves and Their Work

3. POOR: A Participant-Observation Study of the Fraternity Initiation Practices of Tau Kappa Epsilon at The Ohio State University
   IMPROVED: Becoming a Greek: Socialization in a Fraternal Organization

4. POOR: "There's No Business Like SNOW Business!": Boy Meets Girl at the Ski Lodge

IMPROVED: Dating Rituals Among College Students at a Winter Resort

The original titles in the first and second examples fail to convey enough information about the research. They are so broad that your readers will not know what to expect in your paper. The third title suffers from the opposite weakness; it is cluttered with detailed information and consequently fails to identify the general social process (in this case, socialization) of which this particular group is an example. The last title is an example of where an attempt to catch the interest of your audience backfires. In general, avoid puns; your reader may not share your sense of humor. Your title provides the first opportunity to win over your audience. Don't waste it.

Center the title in the middle of the first page of your paper. Near the bottom of the page center your name, course number, and date. Don't number this page.

THE ABSTRACT

Because abstracts are discussed in the previous chapter, only a few words are necessary here. Your abstract, roughly 100 to 250 words, should highlight the major findings and contributions of your research. Don't include extraneous material, such as hypotheses you failed to test or sources that were of only minor relevance to your thesis. The abstract should also briefly describe the sampling procedures and methods used. Abstracts are seldom written in the first person.

The following is an abstract from *Social Problems.* Note how the author clearly and succinctly states the thesis of his paper.

The Dangers of Dependency:
New Findings on Domestic Violence
Against the Elderly

Drawing on data from a case-control study of physical abuse of the elderly, this paper examines conflicting hypotheses: (1) that the increased dependency of an older person causes stress for relatives, who then respond with physical violence versus (2) that the increased dependency of the abusive relative leads to maltreatment. The results of quantitative and qualitative analyses are consistent: the elderly victims were not likely to be more dependent, but were instead more likely to be supporting the dependent abuser. These findings have important implications for social exchange theory and for policy towards the aging. (Pillemer, 1985:146)

THE INTRODUCTION

A good introduction sets the context for the rest of your paper by doing two things. First, it places your research within a larger disciplinary framework. It immediately signals how you intend this work to be read, that is, as following a certain theoretical, methodological, or empirical tradition (e.g., "In this study we explore reactions to drinking using an interactionist perspective."). Second, an effective introduction to a research paper offers a clear thesis statement as well as your response to this thesis. Provide your audience with some hint as to what your conclusions will be, leaving a more complete discussion of these for the end of the paper (e.g., "We conclude that responses to public drinking are a function of social distance between the drinker and his or her audience."). All of this should be accomplished in the first few (if possible, the first one or two) paragraphs; journal-type writing does not allow you time to follow a circuitous route to your thesis.

Introductions are frequently organized in "point-counterpoint" fashion. They begin with a general statement assessing the history of research devoted to a particular topic. This generalization may focus on the type of work that has been done or on the findings from this work: "Students of community have long been concerned with patterns of neighborhood change . . ."; "In the past several decades the study of deviant behavior has increasingly focused on the 'medicalization' of deviance . . ."; "The controversy over the viability of the nuclear family continues to rage . . ."; "Previous research indicates a great deal of consensus over the role of economic factors in migration decisions. . . ." The author then takes exception to this general assessment of the field or of a body of research, using it as a foil against which to present the thesis of the paper. The thesis may call attention to the omission of an important variable from previous research ("But few have been directly concerned with the role of X in this process"); or the thesis may challenge the assumptions of previous research ("But research to date has underestimated Weber's depth of understanding of X"); or it may question the methods employed in previous research ("But comparative analysis based on survey results is necessarily misleading").

This type of introduction satisfies the criteria for a good opening to a research paper; it provides immediate clues to your reader about the context and specific focus of your work. The danger in following this format is that of creating a straw man, that is beginning with an invalid criticism of previous research in order to strengthen the impact of your thesis. If you write, "Introduction sociology textbooks describe the mafia as if it were a closely knit organization controlled by a few powerful individuals. Such a picture of organized crime grossly misrepresents reality," then you must be able to support your claim that this generalization holds for *all* introductory textbooks. Consequently, authors often qualify their initial claims so as to deflect potential criticisms (e.g., writing "*Many* introductory texts . . ." or "*Older* introductory texts . . ."). Your readers must agree with your assessment of a body of literature; otherwise, your introduction will create a hostile audience from the outset.

Another way of beginning a research paper is to place your specific topic within a general class of phenomena, describing how you will discuss this topic. This type of introduction is not used as frequently, largely because it does not immediately locate your research within an established body of work. It may nonetheless be an effective way of starting your paper if your focus is largely descriptive or if you are writing about a topic on which little work has been done. An ethnographic study of an urban neighborhood, for example, may offer insights concerning general patterns of social organization. The study, however, may not have been undertaken in response to omissions in previous research. (You may have been given the assignment by your research methods professor.) If something like this is the case, you need not search for a way to use the "point-counterpoint" construction. (Remember the pitfall of the straw man.) Instead, simply begin with a general statement that will frame the thesis of your paper, and then proceed to outline how you will support this thesis.

An example of this second type of introduction comes from Melbin's (1978) "Night as Frontier." Although only the first paragraph of the paper appears here, it provides enough information to show where the author is going:

> Humans are showing a trend toward more and more wakeful activity at all hours of day and night. The activities are extremely varied. Large numbers of people are involved. A unifying hypothesis to account for it is that night is a frontier, that expansion into the dark hours is a continuation of the geographic migration across the face of the earth. To support this view, I will document the trend and then offer a premise about the nature of time and its relation to space. Third, I will show that social life in the nighttime has many important characteristics that resemble social life on land frontiers. (Melbin, 1978:3)

Regardless of which type of opening paragraph you choose, the introduction should include a brief literature review. The review of the literature you write for a research paper is much shorter and more focused than one you would write if the sole purpose of the paper is a review of the literature on a particular topic. (See the previous chapter for help with writing literature reviews.) When you write a literature review that stands on its own, the theme and organization of the review flow from the broad themes you identify in the library materials you read. When you incorporate previous research into a research paper, you select the literature for its relevance to your particular thesis or set of hypotheses.

Because space limits what you can present, carefully select the literature you cite in a research paper. You will, of course, want to discuss the major studies relevant to your topic, but how do you gauge the relative significance of published research? One way is to see if the article is often cited in the work of others. How many entries are listed below it in the *Social Sciences Citation Index* (see Chapter 6, "Using the Library")? How many of the articles you have collected refer to it? Another way of assessing a study's significance is to look at where it was published. Did it appear in one of the leading journals in its respective discipline? (It will take you a while, of course, to get to know which journals are the leading journals.) If neither of these approaches works, you might try enlisting your instructor's assistance in sorting out the most important sources. Keep in mind that, aside from the research's scholarly significance, your discussion of previous research is guided by its relevance to your specific thesis. Include only those studies that bear directly on your topic of interest.

Here is an example of an introduction that effectively combines a brief review of the literature with a statement of the thesis of the research.

Rule Enforcement and Moral Indignation:
Some Observations on the Effects of
Criminal Antitrust Convictions Upon
Societal Reaction Processes

The roles of rule enforcement and formal labelling in the process of creating deviant careers has been relatively well-explored in recent years. A second aspect of rule enforcement, however, has rarely been studied—the effects of rule enforcement upon the maintenance of moral opprobrium toward not just the deviant, but also toward *deviant behavior categories.*

Concern with this aspect of deviance originated with Durkheim (1947:102), who suggested that punishment primarily serves to emphasize and reinforce prevalent values. An interesting phenomenon to investigate in light of this thought is the corporate offense, as this category of violation currently meets with weak, unorganized indignation. In the long-running controversy over the essential nature of corporate offenses, both proponents (notably Clinard, 1946; 1952; Hartung, 1950; and Sutherland, 1947) and opponents (notably Burgess, 1950; Kadish, 1963; and Tappan, 1947) of a criminal definition noted that violations in this area are not generally regarded as particularly reprehensible either by enforcement agents or the public at large. A small number of impressionistic and empirical studies bear out this conclusion (Dershowitz, 1961:288–289; Geis, 1968; Newman, 1957; Smith, 1961).

This pattern indicates that the moral opprobrium which initially led to the creation of this class of violations has not endured. A key factor in the neutralization of moral opprobrium toward corporate offenses is the pattern of formal response established in regard to such violations. The following analysis focuses upon the Sherman Antitrust Act, one of the first federal regulatory laws, in order to demonstrate what social phenomena may occur when sanctions are rarely applied to a particular form of deviance. (McCormick, 1977:30)

A few final words should be added about introductions. Make sure to state your research hypothesis clearly and explicitly. Phrase the hypothesis (or set of hypotheses) in terms of the major variables analyzed in your study: "We expect both the number of functional divisions and the age of the firm to be highly correlated with organizational size, as measured by number of employees"; "Length of sentence should vary directly with the number of previous convictions of the offender"; "Even when controlling for variation in social class, the relationship between gender and attitudes concerning the Equal Rights Amendment will persist." The hypotheses you state in the Introduction should provide the organization for the presentation of findings and discussion that follow.

THE RESEARCH METHODS SECTION

The methods section describes how you collected and analyzed the data for your research paper. It should be relatively detailed and should provide a context for the arguments you make in the remaining sections of the paper. The elements discussed in the methods sections include the following:

1. *The sample.* Begin by describing the units of analysis in your study. Are they individuals, collectivities (e.g., families, clubs, businesses, or communities), or artifacts (e.g., television programs, newspapers, magazines, or court cases)? Next, provide a description of your sampling procedures. How did you select your specific sample from this larger population of people, groups, or objects? If you drew a *random sample,* describe the list (e.g., a telephone or city directory, block maps, court dockets, class rosters) from which the units of analysis were selected. Finally, discuss how you selected the sample from this list (e.g., numbering each case and selecting cases using a table of random numbers; or beginning with a random start, and selecting every tenth case). If you

divided your list into two or more groups before sampling (what social scientists refer to as a *stratified sample*), then state your reasons for doing so. For example, if you are interested in an attitudinal issue on which you expect men and women to hold different opinions, but your list of potential respondents contains many more men than women, you may want to use a stratified sample based on sex. In this case, using a simple random sample may not yield enough women to allow for a meaningful analysis employing sex as an independent variable.

If you do not or cannot use a random sampling technique, explain why. In general, randomness in sample selection is more important in quantitative than in qualitative studies because of the assumptions made in tests of statistical significance that allow the researcher to make inferences about some larger population using sample data. Even when randomness is not essential to the goals of your research, it is a good idea to discuss, at least briefly, the *representativeness* of your sample. For example, you might claim that you selected a particular college class for your study of teacher–student interaction because it appeared typical (in size or in proportion of male and female students) of other classes taught at this school.

State the total sample size and, if relevant, the response rate. ("Of the 100 students selected to participate in this study, 83 agreed to be interviewed.") Discuss any problems you encountered in selecting the sample and whether these lowered the level of participation in the study. Finally, briefly describe the sample in terms of characteristics significant to your investigation. If, in a study of community businesses the age, size, and location of firms are important variables, discuss how the businesses in your sample are distributed among the categories of these variables.

2. *The measurement instrument.* After describing your sample, discuss the tools you used to observe and record your data. Did you administer a questionnaire to respondents yourself, or did you mail one to them? Did you conduct an interview face-to-face or over the phone? Was the interview structured (i.e., did you ask everyone the same questions in the same order) or unstructured (i.e., did you allow the answers given by a respondent to determine the course of the interview)? Were both open-ended and close-ended questions

included in the interview or questionnaire? How long did it take to complete a typical interview?

If you conducted a qualitative field study, describe what your observations consisted of. Did you keep a journal based on you-robservations of this group or setting? What kinds of information did you record? If you conducted a content analysis of a set of artifacts, describe what you looked for in each object in the sample and in what form these data were recorded.

Regardless of the particular methodological tool, specify how the major variable in your study is measured. For most research investigations, this will be the variable that you are trying to explain or predict—the *dependent* variable. If, for example, you designed a survey to study alienation in the workplace, you might write, "An additive index of alienation was constructed from responses to five questions, each measuring one of the dimensions of alienation defined by Seeman (1954): powerlessness, normlessness, meaninglessness, isolation, and self-estrangement. A score of five on the index represented the greatest degree of alienation; a score of zero represented the least degree of alienation." If you rely on a measurement scheme developed by someone else, be sure to acknowledge your debt—e.g., "Several questions measuring powerlessness in the workplace developed by Jones (1972) were also asked."

The need to state clearly how the dependent variable is measured is even more imperative when you don't prescribe a fixed set of answers for it. If you use open-ended questions to measure a variable (e.g., "Why did you move to Alaska?" "What does it mean to you to feel 'at home' in a place?"), describe how you developed a coding scheme for the range of responses.

3. *The research context.* Provide any additional information necessary to ground your research in a specific context. When was your research conducted? For surveys, give the dates during which it was administered (e.g., "May through July 1987"); for observational studies, report the time of day and period of observation; for analyses of artifacts, give the time period encompassing your observations. Where was your research conducted? What role did you assume in this research (e.g., did you participate in the life of the group or did you simply observe)? You might also forestall criti-

cism by discussing any problems you encounterd in collecting your data, such as incomplete records from which to work or an inability to observe certain behaviors.

Don't feel that you have to discuss each of these elements of your research strategy in the order I have presented them. It is more important that your discussion address clearly the range of methodological issues outlined here. The following methods section from a paper describing what people think about city life is a good example of how a writer can briefly cover this range. (The passage in the original paper is even more descriptive than it appears, because several footnotes printed in the original are omitted here.)

> To explore such complex patterns of belief and sentiment about cities, 77 adults were interviewed in four communities in northern California: San Francisco, a central city; Hillcrest, an upper-middle-class suburb; Bayside, a working-class suburb; and Valleytown, a rural small town of 7,500 in California's central valley. The names of the smaller communities are fictitious. These four communities do not represent the total diversity of community life in contemporary America, nor is each community typical of all communities of its type. However, this *comparative* sample of communities facilitates documentation of views toward urban life in different community contexts and, through comparison, a better appreciation of the range of urban views across community forms (Glaser and Strauss, 1967).
>
> Households in each community were selected randomly from dwelling lists in two or more theoretically chosen neighborhoods. Using census tract data and field observation, middle- and working-class neighborhoods were designated in each community to ensure class diversity within each community type. Given the racial segregation of suburban and small-town communities in northern California, particularly excluding blacks, the San Francisco neighborhoods selected were composed predominantly of white residents. This ensured that urban residents did not differ significantly in minority background from suburban and small-town residents. Households were sent a letter describing the research; up to four call-backs were made to locate residents and this led to slightly over half of the selected households.
>
> The interview focused on issues of community belief and sentiment and utilized open- and closed-ended questions. The former were emphasized to ensure considerable spontaneity, complexity, and richness in responses. Interviews typically lasted one hour and

fifteen minutes and, with the permission of the respondents, were taped and transcribed for analysis. With respect to beliefs about cities and other forms of community, respondents were asked first to describe the form of community in which they resided, based on their designation of that community, and then to characterize other types of communities. With respect to community preference, respondents were asked to select the type of community in which they would most and least like to live from the following alternatives: city, suburb, small town, farm, countryside, or wilderness. (Hummon, 1986:5–7)

THE RESULTS SECTION

This section is often the largest part of a research paper. When you present your findings, you are answering the questions posed by your research hypotheses. An effective discussion section builds a strong case either in support of or in opposition to these hypotheses and sets the stage for the interpretations of the data you provide at the conclusion of your paper.

Avoid the temptation to describe your research project chronologically ("First, I did this; Then, I did this"). Obviously, this is how *you* experienced it, but it is not how you should write about your research. Organize the results of your research around the hypotheses you state in the Introduction. If, for example, your research hypothesis is "Career aspirations are a function of socioeconomic status, race, and sex," then discuss the results of your analysis in three sections: one in which you describe the effects of socioeconomic status on career aspirations, one in which you describe the effects of race, and one in which you describe the effects of sex.

The form in which you present your research findings depends on your methodological approach. If your study is primarily quantitative, your discussion will probably include tables or figures summarizing a large quantity of numerical information. If, on the other hand, your study is primarily qualitative, you will probably organize your discussion around typologies or stages in a process that emerge from your observations. Because of this difference in approach, I discuss these two types of writing separately.

Presenting Quantitative Data

Tables and figures, properly constructed, convey a large amount of information in a small space. They should enlighten, not confuse, your reader; consequently, think seriously about the best way to present them. Tables vary in format depending on what kind of information you collect and what statistical techniques you use (e.g., frequency distributions, cross-tabulations, regressions), but the following general points are useful to keep in mind as you construct any kind of table:

1. *Provide enough information in the table so that it can be read on its own.* Number tables consecutively and give each an appropriate title. Tables should make sense to the reader apart from the text. The title should describe the variables that appear in the table, as well as the type of data that are being presented: "Degree of Financial Satisfaction by Gross Annual Income" (the word *by* connotes a cross-tabulation, i.e., a table containing the joint frequency distribution of two variables); "Marital Status of Respondents in the Sample"; "Standardized and Unstandardized Regression Coefficients for Workplace Characteristics in an Equation Estimating Worker Alienation"; "Mean Levels of Education for Respondents Stratified by Sex and Hours Worked per Week." Avoid computerese in naming the variables used in the title or elsewhere in the table. It makes infinitely more sense to your audience to read "Attitudes Toward Racial Integration by Residential Neighborhood by Race" than to read "RACEINT by NEIGH by RACE."

In addition to giving clear, informative titles and variable names, explain anything that could be difficult to understand in the table. Use footnotes to explain how variables were measured and how indexes were constructed, or to identify the source of the data, if such matters are unclear from the title.

2. *Standardize the format of the tables.* There is no single right way to set up tables, but try to select a format for each kind of table and stick with it throughout your paper—present all cross-tabulations using the same format, all frequency distributions using the same format, and so forth. Place each table on a separate page and cue it into the text using a note such as the one appearing in the following example. Then, collect the tables and append them to the end of your paper.

We were initially interested in the effect of a respondent's religious affiliation on his or her attitudes con-

[Table 1 about here.]

cerning a woman's legal right to an abortion. As Table 1
shows, Protestants are much more likely than either Catholics or Jews to support the legality of abortion.

3. *Discuss tables in the text; don't repeat them.* For example, if
you write, "Men constituted 55% of the sample, women, 45%,"
do not include a frequency distribution of sex in your paper. To do
so would not tell your readers anything they didn't already know.

So what do you write about when discussing a table? The text
of the discussion section should guide the reader through the tables.
You might wish to point out *trends* in the table. As you move across
categories of the independent variable, what happens to the dependent variable? What are the modal categories (i.e., the ones with the
greatest frequencies) in the table? Or you might wish to *highlight*
the more theoretically or empirically interesting findings in the
table. Why are some variables in the equation statistically significant and others not? Why are almost all of the observations con-
centrated in the extreme diagonal corners of the table? You don't
have to discuss everything that appears in a table, but you must
make sure that the table, as a whole, warrants inclusion in your
paper. Almost worse than repeating in the text the information in
a table is including a table that you fail to mention in the text.

4. *Be selective in choosing tables to include in your paper.* Too
many tables—especially those displaying findings that can be easily
described in the text—both confuse and fail to impress your readers. A few well-chosen and properly constructed tables can provide
the basis for a thoughtful and effective research paper.

CONSTRUCTING FREQUENCY DISTRIBUTIONS

A frequency distribution reports the outcome of a single variable in terms of its categories. If we wanted to construct a frequency distribution of marital status, for example, we might place
everyone in the sample into one of five categories—"married,"
"divorced, "separated," "widowed," or "single/never married"—
and then tally the number of persons in each category. The categories of variables reported in properly constructed frequency dis-

tributions are both *exhaustive* (i.e., every element in the sample is placed into some category) and *mutually exclusive* (i.e., no element is placed into more than one category.) For the variable of marital status, this means that, at a given point in time, no one would fail to be accurately described by one of these five categories of marital status (exhaustiveness) and that no one possesses more than one of these marital statuses at one time (mutual exclusiveness). Adding the number of cases in each category results in the total sample size.

Percentage frequency distributions are created by dividing the number of scores in each category by the total sample size and then multiplying each proportion by 100. This has the result of standardizing for sample size and provides a measure more useful in analyzing the data. To return to the preceding example, knowing that 10 men and 12 women were divorced would interest a researcher only to the extent that these values represent some percentage of the total number of men and women in the sample. For that reason, a table of the distribution of a variable usually shows both the number and percentage in each category.

One general format for displaying frequency distributions appears in this table of years of education:

Table 1. Education of Respondents in the Sample

Education (years)	Percentage (N)	
0-11	15.5	(20)
12	34.9	(45)
13-15	25.6	(33)
16-20	24.0	(31)
Totals	100.0	(129)

This table shows the number of scores in each category in parentheses after the category percentages, with the total sample size (129) displayed next to the percentage total of 100 percent. An optional format would exclude the actual number in each category, as these can be calculated by multiplying the category percentage by total sample size.

Missing data (e.g., when a respondent refuses to answer a question or when a question is left blank) are not ordinarily included in the presentation of a frequency distribution. The number of responses defined as "missing" by the researcher is subtracted from the total sample size, and category percentages are then based on the remaining number of responses. An exception to this general rule is warranted when what is normally considered "missing data" is itself the subject of investigation. A substantial lack of response to a particular item on a questionnaire may indicate either that a question is difficult to understand or that it deals with an issue too sensitive to elicit a response. In these cases you might be interested in the number of people that failed to answer the question because it might tell you something about your methodological approach.

Frequency distributions are often described in terms of two summary measures: *central tendency* and *dispersion.* Three measures of central tendency are commonly used to describe the middle of a distribution, although they differ in how that "middle" is defined. The *mode* is a frequency-based measure defined as the category with the highest number of scores. (For Table 1, the mode is 12 years.) The *median* is a positional measure defined as the value that divides an ordered frequency distribution into equal halves. (For Table 1, the median is 12.59 years.) The *mean* is an arithmetic measure defined as the sum of all the scores in the distribution divided by the total number of scores. (For Table 1, the mean is 12.95 years.)

Given that you can describe a distribution in these three ways, which statistic should you report in your paper? Your choice of an appropriate measure of central tendency is constrained by how a particular variable is measured. A median can be meaningfully interpreted only if your data can be ordered from lowest to highest. The categories of variables such as social class, political ideology, and occupational prestige can be rank-ordered, but the categories of variables such as religion, ethnicity, and sex cannot. Thus, the median is an appropriate measure of central tendency for the first group of variables, but not for the second. Similarly, it does not make sense to compute a mean for a distribution unless the categories of your variable are separated by a standard unit of measurement, allowing them to be meaningfully added to or subtracted from one another. Income measured in dollars or education measured in years are both examples of variables for which a mean would be a useful summary measure. Finally, a mode can be computed for any variable, as it simply represents the category with the highest number of scores.

Assuming that the data in Table 1 were originally measured in terms of actual number of years of education completed (before being grouped into the four categories shown here), you should probably report both the mean and median values for the distribution. If these two statistics are close in value, the distribution is relatively symmetric (i.e., the positional and numerical averages of the distribution coincide). If the median diverges substantially from the mean, the distribution is skewed. The mean, because it takes every score into account, is affected by extremes in the distribution. A few high or low scores in a distribution pull the mean up or down, respectively. The median, because it focuses only on the positional middle of the distribution, is not similarly affected by extreme scores. Because the mean (12.95) and median (12.59) in Table 1 are relatively close, you would not conclude that skewness was a problem in this distribution of years of education.

Measures of dispersion quantify the spread of scores about some central value in a distribution; they give us some idea as to whether the outcomes in a distribution are relatively homogeneous (similar in value) or relatively heterogeneous (different in value). The two most commonly reported measures of dispersion—the variance and the standard deviation—represent the scatter of scores about the mean. The variance (s^2) is computed by taking the difference of each score from the mean, squaring these differences, summing them over all scores, and then dividing by $(N - 1)$. The standard deviation (s) is simply the square root of the variance. High values for either s^2 or s mean that the scores in the distribution are widely dispersed about the mean; low values indicate a relatively tight cluster of scores about their mean. For Table 1, the variance is 0.66, the standard deviation 0.82. (By themselves, the numerical values of s^2 and s are difficult to interpret. When compared with other distributions or used in statistical tests of hypothesis, these measures of dispersion are easier to understand.)

Measures of central tendency and measures of dispersion are presented either in the text that accompanies the table or in the table itself. If you choose to include these statistics in the table, place them at the bottom after the frequency totals.

CONSTRUCTING CROSS-TABULATIONS

Because frequency distributions describe the outcome of a single variable, they can sometimes be introduced in the text of a research paper, eliminating the need to present the data in a table. Once you begin to examine the interrelationship of two or more variables, however, the usefulness of tables as summarizing tools greatly increases. Cross-tabulation is one of the fundamental approaches to exploring the covariation of two or more variables when each variable contains relatively few categories. The qualification "relatively few categories" is important. To illustrate, cross-tabulating a ten-category variable with another ten-category variable would yield a table of 100 cells. Not only is such a table difficult to interpret, but unless you have collected a tremendous amount of data, many of the cells in the table are likely to be empty. Whenever you construct a cross-tabulation that results in many empty cells, you should think seriously about regrouping your variables into fewer categories.

Suppose you are interested in the relationship between two major categories of religious preference (Protestant versus Catholic) and two major categories of political party affiliation (Democrat versus Republican). You might construct the following cross-tabulation based on the results of your sample data:

Table 2. Political Party Affiliation by Religious Preference

Party Affiliation	Religious Preference (%)	
	Protestant	Catholic
Democrat	58.4	71.6
Republican	41.6	28.4
Totals	100.0 (85)	100.0 (31)

Table 2 conforms to a general format for constructing cross-tabulations: array the independent variable across the top to establish *columns* of the table, and array the dependent variable down the side to establish *rows* of the table. Then percentage *down* columns and read *across* rows. This rule for constructing the table assumes that it makes sense to think of one variable as "dependent" and another as "independent." (In Table 2, we could justifiably argue that religious preference affects party identification, and not vice versa.) Where this is not the case, the placement of the variables is unimportant.

Does religious preference affect party identification? Reading across the row for Democrats, we find that Catholics are more likely to be Democrats than are Protestants (72 percent compared to 59 percent) and, conversely, reading across the row for Republicans, that Protestants are more likely to be Republicans than are Catholics (42 percent compared to 28 percent). Although the percentage differs between these two groups, the majority of both Catholics and Protestants are nonetheless Democrats.

These results would lead you to conclude that there is indeed an association between religious preference and party affiliation. If there were no association between these two variables, the table would have looked like this:

Table 3. Political Party Affiliation by Religious
          Preference

Party Affiliation	Religious Preference (%)	
	Protestant	Catholic
Democrat	62.1	62.1
Republican	37.9	37.9
Totals	100.0 (85)	100.0 (31)

In Table 3, knowing a person's religious preference tells us nothing about his or her party affiliation. Protestants are just as likely as Catholics to be Democrats (62 percent of both groups); Catholics are just as likely as Protestants to be Republicans (38 percent of both groups). When we obtain these kinds of results, religious preference and party affiliation are said to be *statistically independent.*

A Chi-square (χ^2) test for statistical independence compares the results of a table constructed from observed data (analogous to Table 2) with those of a table constructed from theoretical data that assumes there is no association between the variables under construction (analogous to Table 3). The details of this test would carry us beyond the purpose of illustration here. It will suffice to say that if the divergence between the two tables is unlikely to have resulted from chance factors (e.g., random differences in sample outcomes), then the association between the variables in the table is said to be *statistically significant*. The likelihood that a sample outcome differs from one we would expect given no association is represented in a probability attached to a calculated value of χ^2. In general, the larger the value of χ^2, the more likely it is that the relationship between the variables in the table is statistically significant.

To return to the illustration of religious preference and party affiliation, the calculated value of χ^2 in Table 2 is 16.82. The level of significance associated with this value of χ^2 is $p < 0.001$. This means that it is extremely unlikely—less than a 1 in 1000 chance—that our sample results represent random variation from a theoretical distribution assuming no association. By convention, social scientists are not willing to accept a sample outcome as statistically significant unless its probability of occurrence in a theoretical distribution of no association is less than 5 times out of 100 ($p < 0.05$). Significance levels (either 0.05, 0.01, or 0.001) are always reported alongside calculated values of χ^2 (e.g., $\chi^2 = 5.73$, $p < 0.05$).

Presenting Qualitative Data

The analysis of qualitative data focuses on a thorough description of the organization and varieties of some facet of social life. This does not mean that qualitative analyses ignore the frequency with which certain behaviors occur, only that they pay far more attention to the nuances of behavior that, when reported, provide a rich description of social life. How you present the findings of qualitative research depends on the goal of your research. Qualitative methods are well suited to answering many types of research questions, but they are most often used in one of three ways: (1) to identify the variation in responses to some phenomenon (e.g., the roles inmates adopt inside prisons); (2) to identify the stages in a process (e.g., how someone enters a deviant subculture); or (3) to identify the social organization of a specific group or setting (e.g., how families develop a division of labor). Regardless of the particular focus of the research, qualitative analyses strive to reveal patterns—typical ways in which things happen—in a complex set of behaviors or settings. When they succeed, they often give the reader a sense of having direct experience with some aspect of social life.

IDENTIFYING RESPONSE PATTERNS

One way to organize qualitative data is to construct a typology of responses that exhausts all of the observations you have made. This is an *inductive* approach, arriving at general patterns from the analysis of specific data. For example, Sykes and Matza (1957) were interested in how delinquents justify their deviance in terms that are not always recognized as legitimate by others. Their research resulted in a typology of five rationalizations that delinquent boys used to "neutralize" an image of themselves as deviant:

1. The denial of responsibility ("I didn't mean it.")
2. The denial of injury ("I really didn't hurt anybody.")
3. The denial of the victim ("They had it coming to them.")
4. The condemnation of the condemners ("Everybody's picking on me.")
5. The appeal to higher loyalties ("I didn't do it for myself.")

This typology provides a unifying framework for describing a number of seemingly disparate responses that delinquents gave to justify their behavior. Its general utility has been seen in its extension to descriptions of rationalizations in other settings.

IDENTIFYING STAGES IN A PROCESS

Research papers that focus on processes can often be organized chronologically. In telling your story from beginning to end, you break down what may appear to be a continuous process into critical stages or "turning points" in this process. You may be interested, for example, in what it means to become a member of a group, leave a community, learn a new skill, or end a marriage. Although everyone's experience is not the same, your goal is to identify the characteristics of such a process that are shared by most of the people you observe.

An example of this type of qualitative research is Vaughan's (1986) study of how people make transitions out of intimate relationships. From a large number of in-depth interviews with people at different points in this transition, Vaughan identified several stages in this process she refers to as "uncoupling." She argues that regardless of whether the couple were married or living together, gay or straight, one can locate pivotal points in the process of "uncoupling":

1. *Secrets*—One person (the initiator) begins to feel dissatisfied with the relationship, and in response to this dissatisfaction, starts to imagine a life apart from his or her partner.
2. *The display of discontent*—The initiator defines the partner as undesirable, and in publicly conveying this information, legitimates leaving the relationship.
3. *Mid-transition*—The initiator explores alternative lifestyles that might replace his or her current coupled relationship.
4. *Signals, secrecy, and collaborative cover-up*—Both partners refuse to confront directly the problems in their relationship, thereby cooperating to help each other save face.
5. *The breakdown of cover-up*—The initiator, either directly or indirectly, forces the partner to confront the troubled relationship.
6. *Trying*—The partner urges the initiator to negotiate to save the relationship; the initiator, however, may feel that he or she has already tried to remedy a bad situation.
7. *Going public*—The response of friends and family members to hearing about the troubled relationship diminishes the coupled identity and reaffirms the separate identities of the partners.
8. *The partner's transition*—The partner begins to do what the initiator has done long ago: redefine oneself in terms apart from the relationship.
9. *Uncoupling*—Having arrived at ways of understanding the dissolution of the relationship, both initiator and partner go on to explore their new lives and their altered relationship to others.

Although her research focused exclusively on intimate relationships, Vaughan's analysis can help us understand how people make other life-course transitions. The general stages in the process of leave-taking she identifies may appear when people leave jobs, schools, neighborhoods, churches, or families.

IDENTIFYING SOCIAL ORGANIZATION

How do groups exert control over their members? How do residents define and respond to neighborhood problems? Qualitative analyses seek answers to questions like these by describing the norms and behaviors that govern life in a particular setting. The goal of this type of research is to expose the interrelationships among actors that locate them in some system of organized activity.

In her study of communal organizations, Kanter (1972) was interested in why some utopian communities fail and others succeed. After cataloging the specific practices of a sample of utopian communities, Kanter classified these practices into six categories of "commitment mechanisms" that serve either to detach group members from a previous world or to attach them to a new community. The success of a particular utopian experiment was correlated with the group's ability to secure its membership through a number of these commitment mechanisms. Kanter's analysis yielded the following typology:

Detachment mechanisms:

1. Sacrifice—giving up something as a requirement for membership.
2. Renunciation—turning your back on the outside world.
3. Mortification—stripping the identity of ties to a previous life.

Attachment mechanisms:

1. Investment—committing resources to the group, making leaving costly.
2. Communion—emphasizing the characteristics shared by group members.
3. Transcendance—instilling a strong ideology that stresses the importance of communal life.

Like the other studies described earlier, Kanter's analysis is useful because it sheds light on a general aspect of group life—in this case, commitment. Although her data were drawn from a particular type of group, the typology of commitment mechanisms Kanter constructed from these data tell us something about how groups in general encourage a sense of belonging among their memberships.

Qualitative data usually consist of either field notes or direct quotations from interviews. If your instructor doesn't give you guidelines for presenting these data, here are some suggestions you might find helpful:

1. *Indent and single space long verbatim quotations for field notes.* This format separates your observations from your discussion of them.

2. *Provide a context for your observations.* If you are studying the interactions of members in a particular group, give some background information that prepares your audience for your analysis. You may want to explain why and how the group started, the variation in sex, race, or class in its membership, or its relationship to other groups. If you are writing a paper in which it makes sense to include verbatim quotations, identify the respondents by social characteristics that are significant to your research. For example, if you ask people questions about how they manage neighborhood disputes, you might want to identify quotations in terms of the person's sex, age, occupation, and length of residence in the neighborhood. Make sure you do not "overidentify" respondents to the extent that their anonymity is compromised. Do not, for example, identify a quotation by a respondent's street address or specific job title (e.g., Vice President of Research and Development, Digital Corporation, Maynard, Massachusetts). Place any identifying information in parentheses at the end of the quotation:

> I really don't know when I first sensed that there was a problem with the design of the car. It might have been when the product safety supervisor started complaining about the inconsistent results of the road tests (male, 45, research engineer, 12 years with the company).

3. *Be selective when choosing which data to present.* Like quantitative papers that are cluttered with tables, qualitative papers that are filled with endless field notes or interviews obscure the point of your research. Choose observations for their representativeness: one person may speak for many, or one event may illustrate many different facets of group interaction. The text can then serve as a guide to reading your observations (like with quantitative data) by pointing out the major themes they address.

THE DISCUSSION AND CONCLUSIONS SECTION

The final section of your paper should do two things. It should answer the questions posed in the beginning of your paper, and it should go beyond the particulars of your study to address the broader significance of your research. As you sit down to write the conclusion to your paper, ask yourself the following questions:

1. *Were my hypotheses confirmed?* Did your sample data support or contradict your initial research question, or—a more likely result—are your results somewhat ambiguous? Try to give a reason for any discrepancy between your hypotheses and your results. Did your research design—the sample you drew, the interview schedule you used, the limits imposed by time or budgetary constraints—affect your findings? How could these problems be avoided in the future?

2. *What are my findings an example of?* What do these results, based on data from some particular phenomenon, say about some general social process? The conclusion of your paper is the appropriate place to make generalizations, when appropriate, to a larger group or to analogous situations. For example, what does becoming a member of a sorority say about the general process of socialization in voluntary associations? Of what general significance are the attitudes toward abortion held by a sample of college students? What do the interactions between customers and sales clerks in a department store reveal about the assumptions underlying economic exchange? In demonstrating your ability to think beyond your data to make connections in analogous situations, you emphasize the broader, theoretical importance of your research.

3. *Where do we go from here?* Having provided answers to some questions, what questions concerning your research interest remain unanswered? Research reports often conclude by briefly outlining possible directions for future research. They may suggest, for example, an alternative methodological approach to study the same phenomenon, the inclusion of additional variables into the analysis, or the study of other settings to see if the results of this research can be replicated.

NOTES

If you use any notes in your research paper, number them consecutively and append them to your paper as endnotes. Type them, double spaced, beginning on a new page headed "Notes" (not the last page of the text of your paper). For a further discussion of the content and form of notes, see Chapter 7.

REFERENCES

Collect all references cited in your paper under the title "References" and place them at the end of the paper. Unless you are told otherwise, include only those materials you have cited in your paper. References should be alphabetized, double spaced, and consistent in format. A guide to citation form is given in Chapter 7.

APPENDIXES

Any material that might help the reader to better understand the details of your research may be attached to your paper as appendixes. Measurement instruments (e.g., interview schedules or questionnaires) and codebooks showing how you translated your observations into categories of variables are commonly appended to research papers. Number and title each appendix. (The convention is to use Roman numerals, e.g., Appendix I, Questionnaire for Neighborhood Survey on School Integration.)

Place any tables or figures at the end of your paper, using a separate page for each table or figure. Number and title them, but do not paginate them.

4

Library Research Papers

In contrast to papers based on original research, library research papers (sometimes called term papers) rely on secondary source materials, that is, on descriptions and analyses of social life written by others. Instead of gathering observations or administering surveys, writers of term papers conduct their fieldwork in library collections. I discuss how to find your way through the library in Chapter 6, so here I will focus on how you can shape library materials into an effective paper.

Writing a library research paper is not only a matter of writing; the writer is engaged in an interactive process that alternates and combines writing and research. You will get some idea of what you want to write about—perhaps from a remark in a lecture, or from something you have read in a course—and then you will search for information about it in your library. Maybe you'll take a few notes on what you find. Then you will start to develop a topic and focus your library research. You return to the library for more information and take more notes, but this time you read the materials in a new way. Now you will be reading to test some ideas you have formed about a topic. When you incorporate these new materials into your paper, you may find that your thesis has changed in some important way, so you rework the previous sections you had written accordingly. The point is that you do not simply go to the library, collect all the books and journals you will need, and then sit down to write. You may have to make several trips back to the library and reformulate your initial guesses about the subject several times before you are on your way to writing a coherent paper. All of this means that writing a research paper may take more time than you anticipate, so it is imperative that you get an early start. The day the paper is assigned is not too early to start thinking and jotting down notes about possible topics.

Library research papers assume a variety of forms. They may be open-ended assignments in which you explore some topic covered in a course, or they may address a particular topic specified by your instructor. If you are allowed to select your subject, you might describe some event or public issue and then attempt to analyze it using some general explanatory framework: Who supports "Star Wars" defense research and why? Why did Ford Motor Company sell defective Pintos? What does the public think about the issue of "comparable worth"? What made Henry Kissinger an effective leader? Or you might write an historical analysis of a social institution: How has the Western family changed over time? What lies behind the shift from retribution to restitution in the legal system? What have been the dominant philosophies in American public education in the twentieth century? Or you might write a comparative analysis focusing on two or three subsets of some general phenomenon: Do men and women have different patterns of academic performance? How do Protestants, Catholics, and Jews compare in their attitudes toward legalized abortion? What are the major differences between Western and non-Western childrearing practices? (Of course, you will need to narrow these broad subjects into a workable topic, which I'll discuss shortly.)

As these examples illustrate, the range of possible subjects on which you might write is immense. That is partly why research papers are such an appealing type of social science writing, but it is also what makes them potentially difficult to write well. The first step in writing a good research paper is narrowing the field of possible subjects into a single, workable topic.

CHOOSING A TOPIC

How do you go about selecting a topic for a paper? Many interesting questions will arise while you are taking a course or exploring a new subject, but not all of them can be developed into an effective research paper. As you develop ideas about a topic, ask yourself the following questions:

1. *Is my topic relevant to the course?* Most library research papers are assigned as a requirement for a course, and as such they should be written with the subject matter of that course in mind. You might, for example, write about the causes of crime for both a psychology and a sociology course, but the two papers would focus on vastly different library materials. As you begin to search for a topic, look at the syllabus to see what topics will be covered in the course. Spend a few hours in the library scanning the chapter headings of a textbook on the subject. If any doubts remain as to the relevance of a topic you are considering, ask your instructor. It is to your advantage to find out early in the term whether or not your interest in, say, medieval architecture is an appropriate topic for your paper assignment in Sociology 313.

2. *Is my topic "researchable"?* You may get excited about writing a paper on some topic only to discover that there appear to be few library materials directly pertaining to your subject. Some topics of current interest will not yet have made their way into the published literature of a field. Other topics may be plagued by methodological difficulties, such as problems of access or confidentiality, limiting the amount of research published. Still other topics, such as the role of male exchange students in an exclusively female college environment, may simply not yet have been directly investigated.

This does not mean that you should limit your choice of topics to those on which an obvious body of published work exists. It does, however, mean that you will be required to think more creatively about your particular topic in order to locate appropriate research materials in the library. You must ask yourself the question I posed of research papers in the preceding chapter—What is this an example of?—because doing so may lead you to previous work that deals with analogous situations. Reading about related examples may also help you to analyze your specific example, that is, to frame it in theoretical terms that allow you to break it down into its constituent pieces. For example, if you were writing a paper describing and analyzing the experiences of first-year college students, you might consider how entering college is similar to other transitions—starting a new job, moving to a new neighborhood, or joining a military organization. As you read research reports conducted in these other settings, you may come to see your investigation of college students as an example of socialization into new surroundings.

3. *Is my topic interesting?* While you should always strive to select a topic that will be interesting to your readers, you should attempt, above all, to select one that interests *you*. No matter what topic you choose, you will have to spend a considerable amount of time thinking about it, researching it, and writing about it. If you are bored with the topic, you can be sure your lack of interest will carry over to your writing. This doesn't mean that you should discard a subject because your initial exploration of it failed to capture your attention. It is sometimes difficult to know if something is interesting until you have read a fair amount about it.

4. *Is my topic properly defined, given the structure of the assignment?* The most difficult part of choosing a topic is finding one that can be developed into a paper appropriate in focus and length to the assignment. This entails narrowing a *subject* into a workable *topic* within the constraints of page limits imposed by course instructors or editors of scholarly publications. Suppose you were enrolled in an introductory course in sociology and were asked to write an eight- to ten-page paper about some topic listed on the syllabus. You found the section on community interesting and want to write about experiments in communal living. The subject on which you will write—"utopian communities"—is too broad in itself to serve as the topic for your paper. When selecting a topic, you must narrow your focus to some aspect of "utopian communities," for instance, why these groups were formed or how nineteenth- and twentieth-century American communes might be compared. As you begin to ask yourself what interests or what puzzles you about utopian communities, you are developing possible paper topics. Don't be discouraged if you find, as you explore your subject, that you don't fully understand everything you read about it. This can be a sign not to drop the subject, but to investigate it.

You must, of course, eventually narrow your topic to a supportable *thesis*. (But this is something you should not, or more to the point, cannot, do before you spend some time in the library researching your topic.) A thesis answers some question you pose of your topic. Let's say you begin by wondering why some communes survive while others do not. As you read about communes, you might discover that almost all nineteenth-century utopias were established in isolated, rural areas, while many twentieth-century utopias were started in the middle of large urban areas. If you find that rural communes were more likely to be self-sufficient, and that self-sufficient communes are more likely to succeed, then you have arrived at a thesis for your paper.

It is helpful to ask yourself some questions about your topic before you start your library research. For example, when did researchers first begin to study adolescent suicide? Why does every college senior I know want to be an investment banker? Do welfare programs affect black families and white families in the same ways? Even if you don't pursue these initial questions in your paper, they will give you some place to begin your search for relevant materials. As you look through these materials, however, don't ignore research that fails to address your specific question. You may find that you are more interested in another question that you hadn't considered at the outset.

ORGANIZING LIBRARY MATERIALS

Clear and logical organization is essential to writing a good library research paper. Once you have determined what form your argument will take, you are most of the way there. This is an important difference from papers based on original research. Original research reports (discussed in the previous chapter) can be organized according to the framework of hypothesis testing (i.e., statement of the problem, research methodology, and results). By contrast, library research papers can be organized in many different ways. As you begin to consider the substance of your term paper, you should plan to spend a fair amount of time thinking about how to put it together.

The organization of your paper will be guided to some extent by your subject. If you are writing about a specific event or issue, for example, you will have to begin by describing it in sufficient detail before you can proceed to analyze it. If you are comparing two or three instances of some phenomenon (say, three alternative educational programs), you might begin by briefly describing each, and then go on to discuss their similarities and differences. If your topic is a concept rather than a particular event, you might write about it in terms of several facets, discussing each of these in turn.

A paper on the social-psychological effects of divorce, for instance, might be divided into sections that discuss the effects of divorce on the principals, on their children, on family members, and on friends.

As you collect library materials and think about ways of organizing them, you are performing analysis. You are investigating a whole (e.g., the effects of divorce) by examining separately its several parts (e.g., the effects of divorce on couples, children, family, and friends). Of course, your analysis can succeed only if you have done a satisfactory job of constructing categories into which this information is placed. You must not, for example, write about the library materials in the order in which you locate them, discussing the first study you comb from the library first, the second one, second, and so on. (If this is your approach, you have missed the whole point of the assignment, and you will end up with a weak research paper.) Instead, you must come up with some way of deciding that one particular study should be mentioned first, another last, and still another perhaps not at all or only in passing. As you make these kinds of decisions, you are forced to examine the interrelationships among the parts that together support your thesis and form your completed paper. Although constrained by what others have done (because you are relying on secondary source materials), you are responsible for evaluating and organizing materials that support your argument and accounting for those that do not.

OUTLINING

A good way to construct the categories you will use in your paper is to make an outline. Organizing library materials in an outline allows you to determine quickly what material you have collected and what material needs to be collected. It also helps you distinguish between major and minor issues. And, because outlining requires that you gather, in the same place, references that support the same point, it reduces the chance that your paper will be unnecessarily repetitive.

After you have spent some time researching your topic in the library, sketch a broad topic outline that includes the major points you think you will cover in your paper. Let's say that in a course on organizational deviance you have been asked to write a paper describing and analyzing a specific case of corporate misconduct. You decide to write about the charges of misleading advertising brought by the Federal Trade Commission (FTC) against the Warner-Lambert Company, manufacturer of Listerine. Your initial outline might look something like this:

```
  I. Background of Listerine case
 II. Suit—Warner-Lambert Co. v. FTC
III. Sociological issues raised by case
 IV. Effects of suit on Warner-Lambert
```

This outline suggests that you will begin with a description of the case and then move to a sociological analysis of it. In concluding, you will return to assess the impact of the case on Warner-Lambert. As you continue your library research and the focus of your paper becomes clearer, you refine your initial outline by adding subheadings under each major heading. The result is this elaborated outline:

```
  I. Background of Listerine case
     A. FDA drug efficacy study, 1969
     B. Focus on mouthwash producers
 II. Suit—Warner-Lambert Co. v. FTC
     A. Notification and issuance of complaint
     B. Administrative hearing before FTC
     C. Final order to cease and desist
     D. Appeals—U.S. Court and Supreme Court
III. Sociological issues raised by case
     A. Administrative versus criminal law
     B. Difficulty of establishing intent
     C. Consumers as victims
     D. Organizational stigma
     E. Ambiguity of norms governing advertising
     F. Problems with enforcement of norms
 IV. Effects of suit on Warner-Lambert
     A. Difficulty in assessing impact
     B. Economic impact on Warner-Lambert
```

This expanded outline highlights the major sections of the paper. From the outline alone, one would expect Section III ("So-

ciological issues raised by case") to be the longest and Sections I and
IV ("Background of case" and "Effects of suit on Warner-
Lambert") to be the shortest. (This is probably the way the paper
should be constructed, with greater weight given to analysis than
to description, but I'll return to that in a minute.) As you sit down
to write the paper and review closely the materials you have collected, you might find it useful to do a bit of reorganization. More
knowledgeable and more critical of what you are reading, you will
see with increasing clarity the interrelationships among the issues
you will discuss. With some revision and the addition of library
references, you construct the following outline from which to
write your paper:

   I. Background of Listerine case
      A. FDA drug efficacy study, 1969 (New York Times, 1969)
      B. Focus on mouthwash producers (New York Times, 1970)
  II. Suit—Warner–Lambert Co. v. FTC (Trade Regulation Reports)
      A. Notification and issuance of complaint
      B. Administrative hearing before FTC
      C. Final order to cease and desist
      D. Appeals—U.S. Court and Supreme Court
 III. Sociological issues raised by case
      A. Nature and structure of case
         1. Administrative versus criminal law (Sutherland,
           1977)
         2. Difficulty of establishing intent
      B. Normative dimensions of case
         1. Ambiguity of norms governing advertising (Albion
           and Farris, 1981; Howard and Hulbert, 1973; Walsh and
           Schram, 1980)
         2. Consumers as victims (Trade Regulation Reports;
           McGuire and Edelhertz, 1980)
      C. Enforcement of norms
         1. Problems in judicial interpretation (Advertising
           Age, 1978)
         2. Overlapping jurisdiction of control agents
         3. Organizational stigma

IV. Effects of suit
   A. On Warner–Lambert (<u>Business Week,</u> 1981)
   B. On the advertising community (Stotland et al., 1980)

Note that the original subheadings under Section III have been reorganized and regrouped under three new subheadings. Elaborating this section of the outline identifies several minor points of the author's analysis and reaffirms the central place of this section within the paper. Note as well that the last section of the outline has been changed to reflect the effects of the suit on Warner-Lambert specifically and on the advertising community in general.

A few precautionary words about outlining are in order. Do not allow outlining to become a substitute for writing your paper, that is, for writing effective sentences that are organized into meaningful paragraphs, which together comprise a strong research paper. You can easily spend hours constructing one outline after another (for example, switching points B.1. and B.2., omitting point C.3.), but you will not necessarily write a better paper as a result. You will know what you have to say only after you begin to write your paper (recall my remarks in Chapter 1), and you may well find that some issues you thought you would raise fit more neatly into your outline than they do into your paper. Remember that the purpose of outlining is to *guide* the organization and writing of your paper. Use an outline as a guide—not a prescription—for your writing. If, as you write, it makes sense to stray from the outline from time to time, then do so. If, on the other hand, your paper bears little resemblance to the outline, make sure that your paper still tells a logical and coherent story. (As a test, try outlining it.)

BALANCE

Balance refers to the relative weight of the different parts of a paper. Compared to the number of direct quotations, how often does the author summarize the work of others? How much of the paper is devoted to description rather than analysis? Relative to the rest of the paper, how long is the introduction? These are all questions of balance, and although there are no simple answers to these questions, they require every writer's serious attention. The elements of a good research paper (or any paper, for that matter) are proportional to one another in such a way that the paper, as a whole, appears to be of uniform design and scale. A paper that lacks this sense of balance can cause a reader to lose sight of the author's general point. A three-car garage attached to a one-bedroom house is not unlike a five-page introduction to a ten-page paper.

Balance can affect your writing in many ways, but here I call your attention to three:

1. *Balance between quotation and summary.* Because library research papers rely heavily on secondary sources, they present a strong temptation to quote library materials extensively. You can easily convince yourself that the author of a report you are reading has described the results of his or her research in the best way possible and that, consequently, you should quote the author directly. Such a conclusion is seldom justified. In incorporating the work of others into your paper, you will often find that you want to highlight some points raised by an author and downplay others, or perhaps you will want to mention only briefly a point discussed extensively by an author. In these and many other instances, summary is a much more effective device than direct quotation. On the other hand, if an issue raised in a source is controversial or central to your argument, you may want to quote it directly.

You can look ahead to Chapter 7 for some advice on making decisions about when to use direct quotations. Anticipating the general message given there, you should use them sparingly. Your research paper should not read like a dialogue among published professionals in which you are a detached moderator, interjecting a transitional phrase or sentence here and there. Rather, it should read like an argument you have constructed after thoughtfully reviewing available published evidence. A few well-chosen quotations add support to your argument; too many give the impression that you haven't thought much about what you've read.

2. *Balance between description and analysis.* When instructors assign research papers, they are primarily interested in your ability to analyze an event, an institution, or some other social phenomenon. They are less interested in your ability to describe these things. You will, of course, have to make use of description as you write your paper. For example, if you were writing a paper on the

Listerine mouthwash case outlined above, you would have to describe the action brought by the Federal Trade Commission against Warner-Lambert: What did the FTC find misleading about the Listerine advertising campaign? What did they ask Warner-Lambert to do? How did Warner-Lambert respond? But you need to go beyond reporting these details of the case to show that you can shape these materials into an interesting and instructive narrative. For example, what were the effects of this suit on Warner-Lambert and on the advertising industry as a whole? What does this case tell us about the nature of corporate misconduct? What does it say about the power of the federal government to control large businesses?

While there are no strict guidelines for allocating space between description and analysis, it makes sense to follow one rule: never spend a lot of time describing something unless you plan to analyze it, and as a corollary, spend more time describing those things that are important to your analysis. Lengthy descriptions of particular events or of published research add nothing substantive to your paper; they must be supplemented by an analysis that tells your reader why these descriptive materials are important.

3. *Balance between sections of the paper.* Because they tend to be fairly long, research papers are often divided into sections through the use of subheadings. While helpful in clarifying the organization of a paper, subheadings also provide a guide to assessing the balance between its various sections. They allow readers to compare the length of the descriptive and analytic sections of a paper as well as the relationship of the introduction and conclusion to the body of the work. A thirty-page paper can easily support a three-page introduction; a ten-page paper cannot. In a long paper you will need to give a detailed description of what is to follow, with the object of carrying the reader's interest to the end. A short paper should move more quickly to the point by means of a simply stated opening section.

5

Oral Presentations and Written Examinations

Oral presentations and written examinations, like dinner parties, require a great deal of preparation for what may seem like a brief final product. (Indeed, preparing them accounts for much of the enjoyment and benefit we derive from these activities.) Similarly, like dinner parties, talks and examinations do not normally allow for repeat performances. Once we have taken an examination or given a talk (or a party), we seldom get a chance to correct our mistakes. Consequently, oral presentations and essay examinations tend to produce inordinate amounts of tension, stress, anxiety, and nervousness. Careful preparation, coupled with reasonable expectations about speaking and writing, can help alleviate the unpleasant feelings that may accompany oral presentations and examinations. They also help you get the most out of giving a talk or taking a test.

ORAL PRESENTATIONS

Faced with the need to give a talk, many people can't sleep the night before, have trouble eating, drink too much coffee, and smoke cigarettes—even if they don't usually smoke. Committing thoughts to paper may make us feel vulnerable, but at least there is some distance (in time and space) between us and the reader. When we speak, however, it is impossible to distance ourselves from our words or from our audience.

Much of the anxiety that accompanies public speaking stems from inexperience. Professors in their first semester of teaching are likely to worry much more than their seasoned colleagues about delivering class lectures. But experience explains only part of this difference. In large measure, the success of an oral presentation depends on the speaker's confidence in what he or she is doing. Your confidence will increase if you can answer "Yes" to these questions:

Is my talk interesting?

Is it focused?

Is it pitched at an appropriate level?

Is it the right length?

Do I fully understand what I'm talking about?

Facing these questions and reviewing your plans for your talk become easier the more often you prepare presentations, but they are also questions the novice speaker can—and should—confront in drafting a talk. The discussion that follows should give you some idea of how to prepare a talk, regardless of how much public speaking experience you have had.

Preparing the Talk

1. *Form.* The form of the physical material of your talk—handwritten versus typed, note cards versus typing paper, phrases versus complete sentences—depends on what works best for you. Some of my colleagues prefer to write out most of what they will say, and then practically memorize each page. Others (and I am one of these) use sketchy phrases to outline their talk, making transitions and modifications extemporaneously. I find some sort of outline helpful because it forces me to organize my talk about its main point (more on that in a minute).

Whatever approach you choose, make sure you can easily follow what you have written. Underline or highlight words and phrases, so that you won't get lost in an endless sea of words on a page. Ample margins and indentations can also help keep you on track, and you should write on only one side of the sheet or notecard.

Write your talk in such a way that you are not tempted into a verbatim reading of it. Include enough information to make all of your major points, and if you can't remember an aside or a comment, write it down; don't rely on your memory. But don't be so rigid that you become flustered if you use a preposition or adjective other than the one in your notes. Allow for some discrepancy between what you have written and what you say.

2. *Audience.* Who will be attending your talk? How much will they know about your topic? What points are likely to interest them? What are their expectations for time limits or questions for your presentation? It is often difficult to arrive at straightforward answers to these questions before delivering your talk. You may not know exactly who will attend your presentation, or worse yet, you may know that the range of familiarity and interest in the topic among those in the audience varies widely. A friend of mine who recently interviewed for a position at a liberal arts college was told to give a 45-minute presentation that both students and faculty members would attend. She was told that her talk should "both convey the importance of her current research to the faculty and, at the same time, be accessible and of interest to the students." Much of the anxiety she experienced before her interview concerned how she would produce a talk that would be somewhere between a paper delivered at a professional meeting and a lecture prepared for a class of undergraduates.

My friend decided to orient her talk primarily toward the students rather than the faculty. In writing her talk, she drew on a paper she had published in a scholarly journal, but she omitted many of the technical aspects of her research (e.g., regression equations), provided additional background information and examples that did not appear in the original paper, and defined many concepts that were probably familiar to a professional audience. The decision to make some thoughtful assumptions about your audience is usually a wise one. (My friend got the job.) Your audience is there to learn something; your task is to educate, not to impress.

A final note: try to use examples with which your listeners can identify. When you offer an example, it should evoke a response something like "Oh, yes, that's happened to me (or to someone I know)," "I *did* feel that way," or "I remember reading about that. . . ." To illustrate, assume that you are speaking to a group of students in a college seminar about how people come to feel comfortable in new surroundings. You might introduce this idea in the following way:

> Do you remember your first week of college? If your experience was anything like mine, you were probably overwhelmed by how strange everything appeared. Your roommates, your instructors, your dorm room, your classes—everyone and everything was new. Being in unfamiliar territory, you had to ask a lot of questions: Where is College Hall? Who do I talk to about changing my course schedule? When does the dining hall open for lunch? By the end of the first semester, these and other questions had become part of your taken-for-granted knowledge about your school, and you may have already begun to feel that you "belonged" here by that time. Starting college is one example of a general process I want to talk about today: how people become familiar with new surroundings.

What if you were preparing a talk on the same topic for the same audience, but instead chose the following example?

> Do you remember your first extended vacation abroad? If your experience was anything like mine, you were probably overwhelmed by how strange everything appeared. The language, the food, the customs, the people—everything and everyone was new. Being in unfamiliar territory, you had to ask a lot of questions: Where is the nearest bus stop? What time do the restaurants open for lunch? How much does a taxi ride cost? By the end of the first couple of weeks, these and other questions had become part of your taken-for-granted knowledge about this country, and you probably felt much less of a foreigner by that time. Living abroad is one example of a general process I want to talk about today: how people become familiar with new surroundings.

How many in your audience will share the experience described in the second example? Not many, I would guess—unless you are speaking to a group of Americans in Tokyo. The first example of starting college is much more likely to conjure up familiar images that will immediately draw your listeners into your topic.

Selecting examples that are familiar to your audience does not exclude the possibility that your talk may elicit a response of "I hadn't thought of it in those terms before." On the contrary, ironies or counterintuitive interpretations are often the major strength of a paper or presentation. Relevant examples lay the foundation for these surprise endings.

3. *Content and organization.* Writing can be more subtle and complex than speaking because a reader can go back, if necessary, to reread a dense passage. To put it another way, readers exert greater control over what they read than do listeners over what they hear. Readers can regulate the tempo of the information they receive, return to passages that require a second (or third) reading, or even modify the order of what they read (Chapter 7 before Chapter 3). In contrast, listeners get only one chance to follow the argument of an oral presentation. All of this is to say that good written essays do not necessarily make good oral presentations, and you have to take several differences into account as you begin to write your talk.

First, good talks usually make fewer points—and they make them with more elaborate illustrations of each point—than papers. If you are giving a talk from a paper you have written, the best way to begin is to read it through and ask yourself: What is the point of this paper? Then, go back through a copy of the paper and highlight the passages that support or directly relate to this point. Papers are usually full of material that has little place in an oral presentation, such as asides, multiple references, and methodological details. For example, in your paper you may have described four studies conducted in four different societies, all of which support the conclusion that occupations dominated by men are more highly valued than those dominated by women. In your talk, you might present one of these studies in some detail, and either omit or only briefly mention the others. Don't hesitate to purge such extraneous material; you will either have enough remaining material for the talk or you can add material (e.g., definitions of concepts with which your audience may not be familiar or extra examples to illustrate an important point) not included in your paper. Because it is easy to assume that there is only one way of saying things—the way you have already written it in your paper—writing a talk based on a paper is often more difficult than starting from scratch.

Second, just as you can arrive at new ways of conveying the ideas in your paper, you can arrive at new ways of organizing them. Don't become wedded to the organization of your written paper. Your introduction may place your paper in the context of previous research through a series of citations, but this is not necessarily the best way to begin your oral presentation. For instance, the introduction to your paper might include several references to recent scholarly work on single-parent families. But when you prepare your talk, you decide instead to begin with a brief caricature of a parent in such a family, one that you feel illustrates the conflicting expectations and demands these parents face.

Your paper may also focus primarily on the results of your research, but you may decide it would be better to abbreviate the presentation of results and spend more time on what they mean: their interpretation and implications. The same holds true of the methods section. Your audience will usually be more interested in your data than in how the data were collected. Keep descriptions of your research methods brief, but be ready to answer methodological questions that may be prompted by your talk.

Third, organize your talk clearly and logically, and be sure to share this organization with your audience. Although it is important in your writing, it is critical in a talk that you explain where you are going and when you get there. Your audience should know whether they are in the middle or near the end of your presentation. One way to inform your audience is to introduce your talk with a sketchy outline that gives away the punch line of your presentation. For example, "I have been spending the past several months doing research on dual career couples. I have been particularly interested in how they manage competing work schedules alongside the constraints of raising a family. My research has led me to conclude that these couples arrive at fairly stable solutions to these difficulties, and today I want to discuss three typical patterns of managing work and family I discovered in my research. The first is . . . ." Later in your talk you can draw your audience's attention back to this organizational framework: "The second of the three patterns is . . . ," and so on.

This kind of introduction follows a maxim handed down to countless students of public speaking: "Tell 'em what you're going to tell 'em, tell 'em, then tell 'em what you told 'em." Such an elaboration of the major points of your thesis might be tiresomely repetitive in a piece of writing, but it is imperative when your audience can look only to you for direction. Reiterating the major points of your talk helps your audience grasp what you consider to be the heart of your presentation.

4. *Time constraints.* Just as the length of a paper—whether it is five pages or twenty-five—is usually specified, so the length of a talk is usually specified. Perhaps it is to be one of three talks delivered in a two-hour seminar, each to be followed by discussion. In this case, it would run about twenty to twenty-five minutes. Or perhaps it is to fill an hour. Obviously, the breadth and depth of detail of your talk depend on the time available.

Always plan a few trial runs of your oral presentation before actually giving it. In general, you speak more rapidly when you deliver your talk than when you practice it. (One response to being nervous is to accelerate your rate of speaking.) If your talk is type-written, double spaced, allow about two minutes per page for presenting it. Notes consisting of phrases will vary in delivery time, depending on how cryptic they are and on whether you allow for questions during your presentation. Most speakers allow some time (roughly ten minutes) for questions either during or after their talk.

5. *Style.* Be conversational. Research papers, even when they contain highly technical material, are intelligible because readers can read through them at their own pace, slowing down to chew and digest the difficult thoughts. Oral presentations, however, have to be caught on the wing, so you should avoid complicated language, concepts, and results that need a lot of explanation. Try to talk in a language that can be easily grasped the first time around. Don't hesitate to use first-person pronouns. In searching for models of effective presentations, think about what you liked or disliked about talks or class lectures you have heard.

If statistical materials are an integral part of your talk, bring along copies of tables or graphs that can be distributed to your audience. Keep these to a minimum, however; you want your audience to be listening to you, not reading your materials. An alternative to distributing materials during your talk is to offer them at the end. (You might say something like "I have copies of these materials if anyone would like to see them at the conclusion of my talk.'') If a simple visual image of something is all that is needed, draw it on the board (if one is available). This helps punctuate your talk as well as clarify any misunderstanding that might arise out of a verbal description.

Giving the Talk

1. *Fluency*. Try not to be nervous. You will be—most of us are—and a little nervousness may help you give a good presentation. (Professors who deliver the same lecture for the tenth time often perform poorly because they are not nervous enough.) If you are too nervous, though, you may speak too quickly or distract your audience with an annoying gesture, such as tapping your foot, swaying from side to side, or shuffling your papers. Taking a few deep breathes before you begin helps. So does making a conscious effort to monitor your rate of speaking.

Above all, make sure you know your subject. Practice your talk at least two or three times before you deliver it formally. Try giving it without your notes. Anticipate questions and weaknesses in what you are reporting. And remember, in just a few minutes, it will all be over.

2. *Flexibility*. Although you should know the major points you will raise in your presentation, try to adapt your delivery to the audience's reaction. Watch what they are doing as you speak. Do they nod approvingly at an observation you just made? (Elaborate on this point.) Do they look confused? (Clarify your point or provide an additional example.) Do they appear to be falling asleep? (Consider cutting short your discussion of the point.) Fine tuning your presentation in ways like these requires that you know your material well. Being able to include additional examples or clarification in an emergency will help you make these transitions if you are not comfortable relying on your extemporaneous abilities.

3. *Clarity*. Emphasize the organization of your talk by giving clear verbal signposts of each major point. Change your tone of voice, pause, or speak more slowly. Make sure your listeners know exactly where you are in your presentation at any given moment. Begin by giving a direct, summary statement of your conclusion, and follow it with an outline of the issues you will discuss to support this conclusion. About two-thirds of the way through, it

may be appropriate to say something like, "I want to devote most of the remaining few minutes to. . . ." As you near the end of your talk, let your audience know you are about to end—for example, by saying, "In closing, I would like to make two broad observations about these data." Avoid transitions, in the middle of your presentation, like "finally," "one last point," and "to conclude"; your audience may wonder why you are continuing to speak.

4. *Answering questions.* If you have done a thorough job of preparing your talk, you will have some idea of what kinds of questions people are likely to ask. Even if you are caught by surprise, you will probably be able to provide a reasonable answer to someone's question. You have been working with your subject for quite a while by now, and that makes you somewhat of an expert. Try to organize your answer to the question as the person is asking it. Keep your answer as brief as possible; don't use the question-and-answer period as an opportunity to give another presentation. If the question is at all complex, repeat or rephrase it for the benefit of your audience, and then go on to answer it. If you don't fully understand a question, ask the person to rephrase it, or try to rephrase it yourself and ask the person if you have interpreted it correctly. If you don't know the answer to a question, say so. You might then ask the questioner how he or she might respond—for example, "That's a very interesting idea I hadn't considered. What do you think its implications are for . . .?"

ESSAY EXAMINATIONS

Few students like to take examinations. At least some of this distaste for examinations is related to a misperception of their nature and purpose. Professors are seldom looking for profound, original insights in answers to examination questions. Even though you may have studied for days, the conditions under which exams are administered usually preclude deeply thoughtful answers. What instructors are looking for is an honest attempt to answer the question, a logical and well-organized answer, and an answer that indicates you have read, understood, and are able to identify major themes in course materials. They want to know that you understand the reading and class notes, not simply that you can give them back on an examination.

Preparing for Examinations

Probably your experience has already indicated that you may learn more studying for the final examination than at any other point in the course. Even if your performance on the examination was not all you had hoped for, preparing for the examination forced you to summarize the major themes of the course, to make connections among what might have appeared a dozen "minicourses" during the term, and to confront your understanding (or lack of understanding) of the course materials directly. The following are nothing more than a set of study hints that will help you get more out of preparing for an exam.

1. Read everything that has been assigned for the course and prepare summaries of each article or book. Ask yourself, "Why was this book assigned for the course? What general issue does this article address? How was this book or article incorporated into class discussions or lectures?" Try to associate the authors of the assigned readings with major concepts discussed in their work (e.g., Robert Merton—"self-fulfilling prophesy," Emile Durkheim—"anomie," Erving Goffman—"total institutions").

2. After you summarize each article or book, think of additional examples that support (or fail to support) the conclusions of the author. Illustrations of your own demonstrate your general understanding of the issues raised in the context of particular studies.

3. Search for connections between course materials. Which studies can be logically grouped together? Which studies offer conflicting perspective or conclusions? If you look for patterns in the readings before the exam, questions that ask you to compare or contrast two perspectives or authors will be easier to answer.

4. Analyze the course. Examinations are not a test of everything you have covered in a course; they consist of a sample of questions drawn from a broad range of topics. Consequently, you

should not be angry with your instructor if you end up studying a lot of material that is not included in the examination. Instead, critically analyze the course to determine what topics are likely to appear on the examination. Which topics were emphasized in the course? Did the instructor focus primarily on theoretical, empirical, or methodological themes in course materials? What did you talk about in class discussions? I'm not suggesting that you draw your own sample of course materials and then study only these. Taking that kind of Las Vegas gamble can easily backfire. On the other hand, you should not study indiscriminately.

Taking the Examination

Although these remarks assume that you are taking an examination with prescribed time limits, they should also assist you in writing a take-home examination.

1. Read through the entire examination before you write anything. If someone is proctoring the exam, ask for clarification of any question you do not fully understand. If you have a choice of which questions to answer, tentatively identify the ones you will complete. I say "tentatively" because later, having answered "A," you may get good ideas for "C," and so go on to answer "C" instead of (as you first thought) "B." That is, while answering one question, you might get ideas for another. (Or, indeed, you may realize that you *don't* have any ideas for a question you intended to answer.) Obtaining an overview of the examination helps settle your nerves.

2. Answer the easiest questions first. You should be able to get through these quickly, leaving time for questions you find more difficult. If you are writing in an examination book, don't feel obliged to answer the questions in the order in which they appear on the exam. You should, however, follow the general framework set forth in the examination. If, for example, you are asked to define five terms and write three short essays, don't intersperse a few definitions between each essay. Instead, allow enough room so that you can place all of the definitions together, even if you do not write them all at once. And be sure to identify, by number or letter, the questions you are answering. Often it is useful to rephrase the question at the beginning of your answer, for example,

> QUESTION: Using a conflict perspective, critically evalu-
> ate functional theories of social change.
>
> ANSWER: "Conflict theorists reject functional explana-
> tions of social change on four grounds. First, . . ."

3. Pay attention to the weight accorded different questions. If some questions are weighted more heavily in the calculation of the examination grade, spend more time (and write more) on these.

4. Read each question carefully. If the question says to "compare," then discuss similarities and dissimilarities among the subjects of the question. If it says "list," then name and describe the appropriate items. (Examples of each item are often welcome additions to lists.) If the question asks for your opinion about something, then give it and substantiate your answer with evidence; otherwise, refrain from casual remarks preceded by "I think . . ." or "I believe. . . ."

It is my impression that when students try to answer questions that baffle them, they often rely on the shotgun approach. Practitioners of this method begin by identifying several key words in the question. They then proceed to write as much as they know about each key word, with little regard for the specific focus of the question. Consider, for example, the following question:

> We have discussed four perspectives of deviant behavior,
> yet it is not clear that they are equally powerful explana-
> tions for a given form of deviance. Do some theories seem to
> be appropriate explanations for only some types of devi-
> ance? Under what conditions is one perspective more useful
> than another?

Students applying the shotgun approach to this question would immediately begin to write down everything they can remember about each of the theories of deviance discussed in the course. Although some degree of background information concerning these theories is necessary to answer the question, an indiscriminate attempt to summarize several weeks of class materials does nothing more than fill several blue books and waste valuable time that might be spent answering other questions. You cannot expect to get full credit for your essay without coming to terms with the heart of the question. (In my example, this comes in the last sentence of the question.)

5. Take a few minutes to prepare a brief outline of each question before writing your essay. An outline focuses and organizes your answer, and once it is done, you have gone more than halfway toward answering the question. If the question asks you to "list four characteristics of bureaucracy as defined by Weber," your outline should consist of four characteristics with cryptic notes (perhaps illustrations) listed under each. If the question asks you to "Compare bureaucratic and nonbureaucratic forms of organization," you might construct a table of two columns across the top (one for each type of organization) and rows down the side for each trait on which you will compare these organizations:

Characteristics	Bureaucratic	Nonbureaucratic
1. Authority	hierarchical	dispersed / collective
2. Rules	formal	informal
3. Division of labor	complex	simple
4. Social relations	impersonal / role-based	personal

6. Despite the pressure of time (you will want to write down everything you know), write as legibly as possible. If most instructors are like me, they relegate the illegible blue books to the bottom of the pile, only to be reopened after mustering a strong resolve to finish grading. In addition to writing as neatly as possible, try other methods to ease the strain on your instructor's eyesight and patience; write on every other line, and on only one side of the page. As I mention in the chapter on form, a messy paper may lead your reader to focus on appearance, not content.

7. Don't assume that your instructor will read between the lines of your examination. Although most instructors give students the benefit of the doubt in ambiguous situations, they are forced to mark examinations on the basis of what has been written, not on what might have been written. They will not assume that you knew more about the question and simply ran out of time or that you could have provided a relevant citation or example but chose not to do so. If you do run out of time before finishing a question, you might conclude with a sketchy outline of the rest of your

answer. This will at least demonstrate to your instructor that you might have written a more complete answer, given more time.

Sample Examination Answers

Here are two answers to a question that appeared on a final examination in an Introductory Sociology class. The question was, "In what ways does Ralph Turner's description of the origins of significant social movements differ from earlier strain theories?" Answering this question requires writing a comparison. The student must first describe "earlier strain theories" of social movements and then show how Turner's theory differs from these.

There are several important differences (in addition to length) between these two answers. The first answer—the weaker of the two—moves too quickly to a discussion of Turner's work. Although the author need not offer a definition of social movements, she should provide a more detailed description of strain theories. Similarly, when the author of Answer A turns to a discussion of Turner's work, she does not provide enough detail about his theory of social movements. Her discussion of redefining the situation as injustice rather than misfortune dominates the remainder of the answer, yet different types of social movements are neither described nor illustrated.

ANSWER A

Clearer exposition of strain theories needed

Earlier strain theories stated that whenever the conditions of a certain group of people got bad enough, they would rebel or revolt and try to change and improve their situation. However, this explanation didn't give reasons as to why, when conditions were bad for an extended period of time, people would rebel at one specific time.

Turner's description varied from these earlier theories in that he argued that in addition to bad conditions, it was necessary for the people in this situation to <u>redefine</u> their situation, labeling it as no longer tolerable.

Generally, Turner explained that this redefinition would come about after an <u>improvement in the people's situation</u>, at which time they would look back and decide that the conditions that they had accepted all along were, in fact, no longer acceptable.

need to be more specific here

The question of redefining a situation has to do with how the situation is <u>perceived</u>. A classic example of this would be "misfortune" versus "fate." In the former, the situation is defined as being bad, but the victim doesn't blame anyone or seek reparations. The situation is seen as something that can't be helped, perhaps a consequence of fate. In the latter, the situation is also perceived as being bad, but it is no longer "accepted," in any sense of the word. It is now perceived as someone's (or something's) fault. Here, some sort of reparation or compensation is due the victim.

What about some examples analyzed by Turner?

With these cases, the reaction of the victim varied, depending on how the situation is perceived and defined ("misfortune" or "injustice.") With a misfortune, the victim does not feel necessarily entitled to help or reparation, and as such, his or her only recourse in seeking such assistance would be to beg or plead. When an injustice is done, the victim feels entitled to such help or reparations, and as such, feels free to demand it.

repeats points from previous paragraph; doesn't add new information

In addition to the problems I have already mentioned, Answer A is somewhat repetitive. The last paragraph does little more than reiterate the issues presented in the previous paragraph.

The second answer, in contrast, begins by defining social movements and summarizing earlier strain theories. It then goes on to describe three previous theories, in each case referring to their authors. After a nice transition at the beginning of the third paragraph, the author provides a fairly detailed discussion of Turner's theory of social movements. She writes about the critical importance of redefining social conditions in the context of three types of social movements described by Turner, offering examples of each type, and concludes by describing the conditions under which these redefinitions occur.

ANSWER B

Many social scientists have attempted to explain social movements, events that occur when people come together

good Succinct Definition

with the intention of bringing about or resisting cultural, economic, or political change. Early strain theories assumed that when enough discontent arises among enough

good Summary

people, the inevitable result is an outburst of some kind. Alexis de Tocqueville suggested that a social movement takes place after a period of strain, followed by a period

relevant examples

of advancement. Once an oppressed people received a taste of "the good life," they would no longer be able to suffer silently. Karl Marx argued that when the peasants become so pauperized, starving and poor that they could no longer

good transition

stand it, they would initiate the Communist Revolution. Building on these theories, James Davis, a contemporary social scientist, claimed that a social movement is likely to occur after a period of advancement, followed by a period of stagnation. Employing the notion of "increasing expectancies," he argued that people would continue to expect more and that when it never came, they would join together in a social movement.

None of these strain explanations accounts for the

important point emphasized

fact that social conditions are bad for some people all of the time. Taking Marx's example, the question could be asked: "Why didn't the peasants, who had been suffering for centuries, rebel sooner?"

good transition

Ralph Turner's description of the origins of significant social movements supplies the answer to this question. Turner felt that strain was not enough: oppressed groups must redefine their situation. Where they once saw their conditions as misfortune—as a fate which they could do little to change—they come to see the same condition as an injustice, brought about by others. When the condition is defined as an injustice, the frequent response is revolt.

detailed information — Turner's theory, coupled with relevant examples

Turner distinguished three types of social movements and the redefinition necessary for them to occur. In a liberal humanitarian movement, such as the French Revolution, people come to see their inability to participate in politics as an injustice. In social reform movements, such as the Communist Revolution, people redefine their lack of material wealth as an injustice. Finally, in contemporary social movements, such as the Women's Liberation Movement, the denial of personal fulfillment is no longer seen as an unavoidable misfortune but as a curable injustice.

good extension of ideas raised in previous paragraph

Turner's theory, after answering the question of why revolt takes place when it does, goes on to explain why the redefinition of social conditions occurs. According to Turner, people redefine their condition when there is a rise in the conditions of the major class without a corresponding increase in other social statuses. This inconsistency propels them to act. In a liberal humanitarian movement, a rise in economic wealth, but a lack of political power, can be viewed as the motivating inconsistency. In social reform movements, greater numbers acquiring jobs but not job security can be seen as a cause. The inconsistency that promotes a contemporary reform movement is a rise in personal autonomy, but a social inhibition to exercise this independence.

Although both of these answers make the same general point, the second answer is more thorough and informative. Providing clear definitions and using well-chosen examples, the author of the second answer has written a significantly stronger essay.

6
Using the Library

No matter what kind of social science writing you do, it will probably require that you devote some time to library research. If you are writing a research paper based partly on work that others have done, you may well spend as much time gathering, reading, and analyzing library materials as you do writing the paper. But even if your writing assignment is confined to materials distributed by an instructor in a course, you may find it helpful to visit the library for additional source materials—either dictionaries or encyclopedias to define or clarify social science concepts, or supplemental studies to provide a broader context for your paper. Time spent in the library is not something you do only *before* you begin to write; it is an integrated part of the process of writing.

This chapter provides a selective overview of the library materials most often used by social scientists. The indexes, bibliographies, and journals discussed here are especially useful to sociologists, although students of anthropology, political science, and psychology may often find the same sources helpful. But before examining the details of social science library research, consider some broad guidelines that may expedite your search for library materials.

SOME GENERAL ADVICE

It is important to approach library research with a realistic set of assumptions and expectations. Even a modest library collection has an enormous amount of "possibly relevant" material. It will take time, savvy, concentration, and—yes—even luck to identify and then get your hands on the specific materials *you* will find useful. It is possible, however, to become both efficient and effective in library research by developing, through use, a familiarity with how library materials are organized and the reference tools that serve as maps for locating those materials. Keeping the following general guidelines in mind may help alleviate the anxiety that often accompanies library research.

1. *Create a schedule and stick to it.* Library research, like all other elements of the writing process, is unlike classroom participation. When you attend a class, you probably participate in a plan devised by your instructor, who has organized the hour, but when you go to the library, you must design your own research plan. What makes library research a creative task is also what makes it time-consuming. Do not be surprised if the number of hours you spend in the library is two to three times what you initially expect.

Why does library research take so much time? Some delays in finding the "right" materials result from the ways libraries operate. For example, you are told to read a book by James McGregor, but when you look him up in the catalog, you can't find him listed. It turns out that your library lists authors whose last names begin *Mc* as though they were spelled *Mac*. You return to the catalog, find the listing for the book, but the book is not on the shelf. You inquire, and you find out that it is on reserve for some other course. All of this takes time, and energy, too.

Or in the course of bibliographic research, you may identify a reference to a journal article or book that your library does not own. A librarian can probably obtain a copy of what you need through interlibrary loan, but there will necessarily be a delay of two or three weeks before you receive it. Similarly, bibliographic searches generated by computers can immediately supply you with a few relevant references, but comprehensive reviews of the literature are usually printed "offline" and mailed to you; a week may pass before you receive the sources on your list. Even when your library possesses the material you need, it may be temporarily on loan to someone else or placed on reserve for intensive use by a particular class. Or something you want (the most valuable reference you anticipate using, of course) may not be where it is supposed to be, and the library staff will need to investigate its disappearance. Or you meet a friend, and chat for half an hour about yesterday's game. Any or all of these possibilities mean that you need to start your research as early as possible.

Delays in library research also stem from the emergent nature of the writing process. When you must select your own topic for a paper, your initial time in the library is exploratory, and very little, if any, of your first efforts may contribute directly to your final paper. You may skim or read many books, encyclopedias, and indexes before you find a topic that both interests you and provides sufficient material for analysis. Even if you have a general topic area in mind, you may still not be familiar enough with the language of a particular discipline to locate useful materials. As a result, you may follow many relatively unproductive leads before you find a path that leads to a fruitful research topic.

Just as half a day is probably insufficient for bibliographic research, half a term is probably excessive. Library research can easily turn into an exercise that becomes an end in itself, rather than a means to an end. It can also provide the researcher with a global rationalization for not writing (e.g., "I don't know enough to start writing yet"). Develop some balance among gathering, analyzing, and writing about library materials. If you are having difficulty knowing how much time is enough, discuss the materials you have located with your instructor. You can always return to the library for additional sources, but you cannot expect to make the best use of what you collect if you are still seeking new material a week before your paper is due.

2. *Keep a record of your library research.* Because it is often impossible to know exactly what materials will be helpful in writing your final paper, keeping track of what you read can save time later on. Documenting your library search need not entail writing detailed summaries of everything, but you should at least make brief notes of materials you find. Be sure to include information on how to relocate these materials; catalog numbers of books are a must, as are the volume number, date, and pages of journal articles.

3. *Develop a research vocabulary.* Like research published in the social sciences, library reference works rely on vocabularies that convey large amounts of information in relatively little space. Thousands of books, journal articles, professional papers, dissertations, reviews, and other research reports enter libraries each year, and keeping track of these materials poses formidable problems. Finding your way through this information requires learning not

one but several methods of arranging information, because research guides do not employ a standard vocabulary or format. Some are compiled by people, some by computers; depending on who or what has done the work, the information available will be more or less cryptic or timely. The description of the bibliographic guides that follows will acquaint you with some of the language of the library, but be prepared to spend some time getting to know how different library materials are arranged.

4. *Ask for help when you need it.* Don't hesitate to ask a librarian for assistance. Although there are broad similarities among libraries, all libraries are not alike. They differ in how their materials are cataloged, where they are stored, how they are obtained (open versus closed stacks, for example), and how and in what form they are kept. More important, libraries differ greatly in their collections. A public library located in a small town may have a collection devoted chiefly to fiction and do-it-yourself books, with very little social science material, whereas a large university library system may have such an extensive social science collection it must be housed in a separate building. Librarians know which materials in their collection will be most helpful to you. Finding out what is available locally is an important first step in library research.

Just as library facilities differ from place to place, the type of research you may be asked to do will change over time. (Again, I don't want to indicate that one can do research only in a large library.) In high school, for example, you may have used a bibliographic index entitled the *Readers' Guide to Periodical Literature.* The range of topics covered and the materials indexed were both broad and general. The *Readers' Guide,* however, will not provide adequate information for a paper written for a college social science course. For that, you need to use other specialized guides compiled primarily for scholarly research in the social sciences.

GETTING STARTED: KEY WORDS AND CONCEPTS

Just as you cannot know exactly what you will say in a paper until you begin to write (and not even then, because you will keep revising what you write), you cannot expect to know what library materials will be best suited to your needs until you begin searching for them. A good place to start is with *specialized encyclopedias and dictionaries.* Unlike general reference works such as *Webster's Collegiate Dictionary* or the *Encyclopaedia Britannica,* these volumes address particular topics within a discipline and provide more than brief definitions of social science concepts. Specialized dictionaries and encyclopedias offer background discussions of the major issues and problems identified with a topic using the language of scholars who write about these issues. Developing a vocabulary relevant to your interests will assist you at a later point in your library search, such as when you look for subject headings in the library catalog.

Specialized encyclopedias can also be used directly in your paper when you incorporate them into your review of major research findings. The entries in these works are prepared by experts who, because of space limitations, usually confine their review to the major, well-documented findings of research in their field. What you read in these reference works is therefore likely to provide basic information.

Finally, entries in these dictionaries and encyclopedias are often followed by selective bibliographies that include many references not directly discussed by the author. You can use these bibliographies to initiate your library research because they will probably include significant research conducted on a topic before the entry was written. Because these volumes are not revised frequently, however, you should turn to other sources for brief overviews of more contemporary research. Recently published textbooks often include such up-to-date bibliographies, as do periodic reviews of the literature, such as the *Annual Review of Sociology.*

For the purpose of illustration, assume that you are enrolled in a class on social problems and that you have been assigned a research paper on any topic discussed in the course. You have a general interest in the sociology of aging and, in particular, are interested in retirement communities.

> Why do people choose to leave their homes and move to age-segregated communities in Florida or Arizona upon retirement?
>
> Are people who move to these communities characteristically different from those who stay behind?

What do people spend their time doing in these communities? Are these migrants happier after they relocate?

You probably won't be able to address all of these questions in your paper, but you have narrowed your topic sufficiently to start for the library. You might decide to begin your library search by looking in the best-known specialized encyclopedia of the social sciences.

International Encyclopedia of the Social Sciences (IESS)

This eighteen-volume reference work discusses the major concepts, methods, figures, and theories of the social sciences. Although it is more specialized in its focus, the *IESS* is similar in appearance and organization to other encyclopedias you have used. It is a useful place to start if you are interested in background information or a broad survey of classical topics in the social sciences; here, you will find entries for important ideas and thinkers, such as "Alienation," "Social stratification," "Community," "Karl Marx," and "Max Weber." Because the *IESS* is not revised regularly—the current edition was issued in 1968—it is not a good place to look for information on such topics of recent professional interest as adolescent pregnancy, family violence, and the effects of the Vietnam War on veterans.

This generalization is borne out in our example of retirement communities. Even though retirement is the subject of many research investigations today, there is no entry in the *IESS* under this heading. Instead, we must broaden our search to include related topic headings, the most obvious being "Aging." Looking under this heading, we find the author's discussion divided into three subheadings: the psychological, social, and economic aspects of aging. A fairly extensive bibliography (again, ending with 1968) is also included.

INDEXES AND ABSTRACTS

Indexes and abstracts are probably the most important bibliographic tools of the social scientist. Like dictionaries and encyclopedias, these reference works are specialized guides to the myriad topics of interest to social scientists. But unlike dictionaries, indexes and abstracts go beyond a brief introduction to a social process or institution; they help you identify scholarly research that has been conducted on some topic in which you are interested. Indexes and abstracts are also likely to be compiled frequently (usually several times a year), so that they contain the most recently published research.

Even if you have never conducted research in the social sciences, you have probably used an index at some time. Your high school or public library no doubt had copies of the *Readers' Guide to Periodical Literature.* Arranged alphabetically by subject and author, the *Readers' Guide* indexes a number of magazines that are of broad public interest, such as *Psychology Today, The New Republic,* and *Scientific American.* These magazines seldom report primary research and, consequently, they are not particularly helpful in writing college-level papers. The research you need will be found in indexes of scholarly journals prepared for different academic fields. You can find this research by consulting two indexes most often used by social scientists, *Social Sciences Index* and *Social Sciences Citation Index.*

Social Sciences Index

The *Social Sciences Index* is the simplest guide to social science journal literature. It is arranged much like the *Readers' Guide,* by subject and author, and is published four times a year and cumulated into annual volumes. To follow our example of retirement communities, we would look for any entries under this or a related heading (Figure 1).

In this issue of the index, there are three listings under the heading of "Retirement communities," the first of which is a comparative study of power and leadership in several communities. The listing gives the author's name (G. F. Streib and others), the journal in which it appears *(Gerontologist),* and the volume number (25), page numbers (403–9), and date of publication (August 1985) of the article.

An entry such as this is fairly unambiguous, because the location of the article *(Gerontologist)* is spelled out completely. Usu-

Retirement communities
   Autonomy, power, and decision-making in thirty-six retire-
   ment communities. G. F. Streib and others., bibl
   Gerontologist 25:403-9 Ag '85
Retirement communities and their life stages. A. J.
   LaGreca and others. bibl *J Gerontol* 40:211-18 Mr
   '85
A wellness program for a life care community. E. L.
   Barbaro and L. E. Noyes. bibl *Gerontologist* 24:568-71
   D '84

Figure 1.   Excerpt from *Social Sciences Index*.

ally journal titles are abbreviated *(Am Stat, Dev Psychol, J Reg Sci,
Q J Econ),* and you must look in the front of the index for a key to
deciphering these cryptic references. If the title of the article looks
promising, all you need to do is determine whether or not your
library subscribes to the journal you need. If your library does not
have the journal, you can probably obtain a copy through interlibrary loan.

Sometimes the *Social Sciences Index* refers you to additional
topic headings. There is no such referral under the topic "Retirement communities" in our example, but under the previous topic
of "Retirement" there is a note to *See also* "Geography teachers—
Retirement." *See also* means that research of *related* interest appears
under the alternative heading or headings in the index. *See* means
that the index uses a heading other than the one you have consulted
to identify research on this topic. For example, under the heading
"Retributive theory of justice" you will find *See* "Punishment." In
the future you need only look under "Punishment" in the index to
find any work that might have been done on retributive justice.

Social Sciences Citation Index (SSCI)

The *Social Sciences Citation Index* is a good deal more complicated than the *Social Sciences Index,* but it is well worth your time
to learn to use it. Because it is computer-generated, the *SSCI* indexes more journals than most other reference works, and it does
so relatively quickly, making it a wonderful source for identifying
recent research. But because it has been generated by a machine,
using the *SSCI* requires that you develop a slightly different ap-

proach to locate research materials. (*Current Contents: Social and Behavioral Sciences,* a weekly publication containing the tables of contents of several major journals, is published between printings of the *SSCI,* providing a guide to the latest research.)

The *SSCI* is divided into three parts: the "Permuterm Index," a listing of entries by subject key words; the "Source Index," a listing of articles arranged by author; and the "Citation Index," a listing of authors cited in footnotes of published work. Each of these is bound as a separate section of the *SSCI.* Using the *SSCI* involves a series of steps leading from one index to another.

The Permuterm Index is the appropriate starting place if you are searching for material on a specific topic. This part of the index categorizes articles according to pairs of significant words appearing in the titles. Because no human judgment intervenes to bring articles on a topic together under broad subject headings, you will spend some time sifting out articles only to find, when you locate them, that you cannot use them in your paper. This is not much of a problem in our example of retirement communities, however, because both words are likely to be used in the titles of relevant journal articles. In the excerpt shown here, the primary term *Retirement* is followed by more than one hundred words that have been paired with it in titles (Figure 2). Looking down the column headed Retirement, we locate the word *Communities* and find that nine persons have written articles in which both of these words appear. The notations appearing after the authors' names provide additional information. A "@" means that this issue of *SSCI* lists more than one article by this author on this topic; a "+" indicates that the "article" is, in fact, a book review. The "▶" before an author's name indicates its first appearance under the primary search term; every other occurrence of this author's name under this primary term will lead you to the same article and, thus, can be ignored.

Looking down the list of other words appearing under the primary term *Retirement,* you can see that searching for useful references is not always so straightforward. For example, is relevant information contained in the article by Belgrave that pairs *Retirement* with *Age-65?* or that by Thornbor, with the term *assets?* Your search may be further complicated by a range of related but grammatically discrete words appearing in the index. Above and below

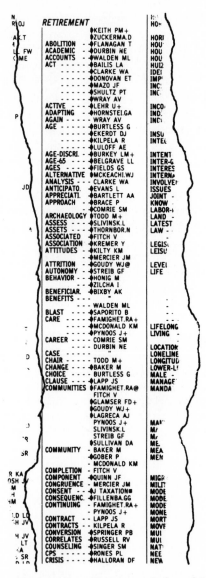

Figure 2.   Excerpt from Permuterm Index of *SSCI*.

the term *Retirement* are listed *Retired, Retired-Worker, Retiree, Retirees, Retirement-Health,* and *Retirements.* Any or all of these listings may contain potentially helpful materials for your paper; the number of leads you pursue is constrained by the time you have to devote to library research. But no matter how little time you may have to spend on the project, begin by considering all of the possible ways your topic might be listed.

Once you have located an entry that seems promising, how do you find out more about it? The next step is to locate the author's name in the Source Index. Suppose you are interested in the article by D. A. Sullivan listed under the paired words *Retirement* and *Communities.* The Source Index listing for D. A. Sullivan identifies two articles (Figure 3). The first is the one you were

SULLIVAN DA
  THE TIES THAT BIND - DIFFERENTIALS BETWEEN SEASONAL
  AND PERMANENT MIGRANTS TO RETIREMENT COMMUNITIES
     RES AGING   7(2):235-250   85   23R
       ARIZONA STATE UNIV,SOCIOL, TEMPE, AZ 85287, USA

ÐUS BUR CENS	73 1970 CENS POP PC23A		
"	83 CURR POP REP P23	120	
"	83 CURR POP REP P20	300	
BARSBY SL	75 INTERSTATE MIGRATION		
BIGGAR JC	79 RES AGING	2	73
"	80 "	2	177
BULTENA GL	69 J GERONTOL	24	209
CHEVAN A	79 SOC FORCES	57	1345
FLYNN CB	80 RES AGING	2	165
FUGUITT GV	80 "	2	191
GOBER P	83 GERONTOLOGIST	23	288
HAPPEL SK	84 AM DEMOGRAPHICS	6	32
HOYT GC	54 AM J SOCIOL	19	361
HUNT ME	82 DETAILED LOOK 10 RET		
JACOBS J	74 FUN CITY ETHNOGRAPHI		
LEE AS	80 RES AGING	2	243
LONGINO CF	79 J GERONTOL	34	736
"	80 RES AGING	2	205
"	81 DYNAMICS AGING		
"	81 GERONTOLOGIST	21	283
SEROW WJ	78 J GERONTOL	33	288
SULLIVAN DA	82 RES AGING	4	159
WISEMAN RF	80 "	2	141

  WEITZ R—OBSTACLES TO THE PRACTICE OF LICENSED LAY
  MIDWIFERY
     SOCIAL SC M   19(11):1189-1196   84   24R
       ARIZONA STATE UNIV.DEPT SOCIOL, TEMPE, AZ 85287, USA

ANISEF P	79 SOCIOL WORK OCCUP	6	353
BALDWIN R	78 WORKBOOK	3	221
BENNETTS AB	82 LANCET	1	11
DEVITT N	77 BIRTH FAMILY J	4	47
DEVRIES RG	THESIS U CALIFORNIA		
"	82 SOCIOL HLTH CARE	2	77
DONEGAN J	78 WOMEN MIDWIVES MED M		
DONNISON J	77 MIDWIVES MED MEN		
LITOFF J	78 AM MIDWIVES 1860 PRE		
MEHL LE	75 BIRTH FAM J	1	123
"	77 J REPROD MED	19	281
"	80 WOMEN HLTH	5	17
NICHOLS E	84 PUBL HLTH REP	99	105
OAKLEY A	80 WOMEN CONFINED SOCIO		
ORTMANGLICK S	78 J NURS MIDWIF	22	39
PEARSE W	76 AM COLLEGE OBSTETRIC		
PETERSON KJ	83 SOC PROBL	30	272
RAISLER J	78 J NURS MIDWIF	22	36
SCOTT WC	80 CONT OB GYN	16	37
SULLIVAN DA	82 MED CARE	20	321
"	83 AM J PUBLIC HEALTH	73	641
VENTRE F	76 BIRTH FAM J	3	109
WERTZ RW	77 LYING IN HIST CHILDB		
YANKAUER A	83 AM J PUBLIC HEALTH	72	635

Figure 3.   Excerpt from Source Index of *SSCI.*

searching for, as it contains the key words of interest ("The Ties that Bind: Differentials Between Seasonal and Permanent Migrants to Retirement Communities"). In addition to the title of the article, the citation includes where it was published (*Res Aging,* an abbreviation of a journal titled *Research on Aging,*) the volume and number of the journal (volume 7, number 2), the page numbers (pages 235–250), and the year of publication (1985). The small print below this information about the article gives D. A. Sullivan's affiliation, followed by the references cited in her article on retirement migrants. These references are listed by author's name, year and place of publication, and page number.

You might end your search for journal articles here, armed with a list of references gathered from the Source Index that leads you to the library journal collection. In the course of your research, however, you might find that articles written by some scholars are particularly useful and that you would like to identify other researchers who have found these articles helpful in their own work. You can do this by exploring the third part of the *SSCI.* The Citation Index lists all of the works written by a particular author that have been cited by other scholars in journals indexed in that issue of *SSCI.* If you want to know who has cited Sullivan's previous work, you would look for her name in the Citation Index and find several entries (Figure 4). The first one looks like this:

```
82  MED CARE    20     321
    SULLIVAN DA      SOCIAL SC M        19   1189  84
```

The information in the first line of the entry refers to an article written by Sullivan in 1982 appearing in the *Journal of Medical Care,* volume 20, page 321. This article was cited by Sullivan herself in an article appearing in *Social Science Monthly,* volume 19, page 1189 in

```
SULLIVAN DA
  82 MED CARE    20   321
    SULLIVAN DA      SOCIAL SC M        19   1189  84
  82 RES AGING    4   159
    SULLIVAN DA      RES AGING            7    235  85
  83 AM J PUBLIC HEALTH    73   641
    SEE SCI FOR 1 ADDITIONAL CITATION
    SULLIVAN DA      SOCIAL SC M        19   1189  84
    WEITZ R          SOCIOL HEAL          7      36  85
  85 EVALUATION PERFORMAN
    HAEMISEG ER      J AIR POLLU        35    809  85
```

Figure 4.   Excerpt from Citation Index of *SSCI.*

1984. If you wanted to find out more about either of these articles, you would return to the Source Index section of the *SSCI* for the appropriate years (1982 and 1984) and look at the listings for D. A. Sullivan. Researching entries in the Citation Index reveals an inter-related network of references, some of which you might have missed in your original examination of the Permuterm Index.

Sociological Abstracts

Abstracts differ from indexes in that they provide more in-formation. As their name implies, abstracts give you a summary of an article as well as its title and citation. Abstracts allow you to judge, with some confidence, which articles will be useful. *Socio-logical Abstracts* classifies research under major and minor subject headings; as you use it, you will learn which headings are appro-priate to a given topic.

Sociological Abstracts also provides a detailed subject index apart from the classified arrangement. In the subject index excerpt appearing here (Figure 5), "Retirement" is the single heading you would need to consult. Reading through the strings of descriptive terms appearing beneath this heading, you will find several prom-ising entries:

> elderly's role alternatives; interviews; Midwestern retirement com-munity; M2682
>
> participant observation; benefits, retirement community example, multiple-methods study; M2903
>
> women/men, support network differentials; gender, marital status; interviews; planned retirement communities, midwest; M2681

Note that the substantive focus of each article, as well as the type of methodology used to collect data, are described in each entry. The numbers appearing at the end of each entry refer to the abstracts found in *Sociological Abstracts,* which are arranged under broad topic areas, but numbered sequentially. The first and third references (M2681 and M2682) are classified under Section 2100, Social Problems and Social Welfare, Subcategory 43, Social Ger-ontology (Figure 6). The prefix for each index number (in these

Retirement
aging women, retirement; work history; S14575
aging, stratification; work, personnel allocation strategies, risks,
   economic structural conditions, retirement; S14116
changing retirement patterns, Paris, France; economic crisis, cultural
   transformations, labor market/retirement income changes; survey,
   industry files; salaried workers; M0990
cost/tenure ratio/faculty flow; mandatory retirement age changes;
   University Southern California Faculty Planning Model; M4542
early retirement, unmarried women; delayed career entry, industrial
   pension structure; longitudinal interview survey; M5862
elderly scientific personnel, labor skills/productivity/retirement, USSR;
   M5185
elderly's role alternatives; interviews; Midwestern retirement
   community; M2682
job deprivation, retirement; older farmers; Iowa; S14709
job redundancy through early retirements, managerial reactions;
   individualistic interpretation, assumptions; L9987
participant observation; benefits, retirement community example,
   multiple-methods study; M2903
pre-/postretirement activities; Jefferson County, Arkansas; S13492
professional athletes' retirement, exit behavior, attitude scripts;
   appropriate/inappropriate performance standards, sociological
   meanings; S13745
retirement adjustment; leisure activity; questionnaire; southern
   metropolitan area; M2679
retirement adjustment; life significance; questionnaire; male managers,
   UK; M6751
retirement as social institution, systems theory; M6749
retirement communities, life history, comparative studies; interviews;
   residents, staff; S15142
retirement, American attitudes; ongoing changes, recent legislation,
   workers/retirees demographic imbalances concerns; content analysis,
   publications, academic materials; S13932
retirement, meanings, problems, responses; social class, retiree's
   resources/value system interaction; questionnaires; elderly subjects,
   mountainous rural area; S14148
retirement, professional activity correlates, interviews; emeritus
   professors, University of Iowa; M4587
retirement, social integration, leisure activities; concrete, symbolic
   aspects, new roles, gender, previous work role; questionnaires; elderly,
   semirural vs urban locations, Switzerland; S14147
retirement; health effects research, Robert C. Atchley's process
   approach; M3701
self-help, volunteer retired physicians/nurses, age peers' health care
   needs; interviews; S15188
sex identity; old age/retirement, personal domains; New York City
   Senior Center; L9851
women/men, support network differentials; gender, marital status;
   interviews; planned retirement communities, midwest; M2681

Figure 5.   Excerpt from *Sociological Abstracts.*

2100 social problems and social welfare

43 social gerontology

82M2681

Longino, Charles F., Jr. & Lipman, Aaron (U Miami, Coral Gables FL 33124), **Married and Spouseless Men and Women in Planned Retirement Communities: Support Network Differentials,** ◆ *Journal of Marriage and the Family,* 1981, 43, 1, Feb, 169–177.

¶ Explored is the nature of informal support given to older persons, depending upon the gender & marital status of the recipient. To control for differential availability of formal resources, random samples of 488 noninstitutionalized residents of 2 midwestern retirement communities were interviewed. It was found that the married have more primary relations than the nonmarried. Married Fs have the most & spouseless Ms the fewest. This deficit is compensated, to some extent, among the unmarried, by the presence of more secondary relations in their support systems. Among those without spouses, the Fs receive significantly more emotional, social, & instrumental support from family members. The greatest informal resource deficits are found among the unmarried Ms. It is suggested that the F investment in maintaining family ties pays off in later life. To a certain extent, the process of resident selectivity may help to explain the differentials in support network. 4 Tables. HA

82M2682

Perkinson, Margaret A. (U California, San Francisco 94122), **Alternate Roles for the Elderly: An Example from a Midwestern Retirement Community,** *Human Organization,* 1980, 39, 3, fall, 219–226.

¶ Increasing numbers of individuals are surviving to retirement age in relatively good health. With the loss of the work role & other roles typically associated with middle age, they are faced with the dilemma of the "roleless role," an absence of well-articulated, age-appropriate expectations & standards of behavior by which to structure everyday life. Recent anthropological, sociological, & psychological studies indicate the possibility of the development of alternate roles & age-appropriate normative systems in age-homogeneous environments. An example of one such alternate behavioral system is provided from data collected by means of interviews with residents (N = 13 Ms, 38 Fs) of a small retirement community in the Midwest. A normative system seems to have developed in which personal qualities such as trust, friendliness, & concern for others are more highly valued than former achievements or occupational status. Residents most frequently cited as having made a good adjustment to aging were not necessarily those who were most active, but rather those individuals who showed a determination to "keep going," lacked self-pity, kept mentally alert & aware, were willing to help others, & showed a sense of responsibility to the community. Various roles were developed & were expected to be assumed by incoming residents: alternate "work roles," represented by committee memberships & volunteer activity; "family roles," represented by the supportive or helping relations adopted toward other residents; & leisure-type roles. These behavior standards & expectations helped to structure the relationships & everyday life of residents within the community. Modified HA

Figure 6.   Excerpt from *Sociological Abstracts.*

examples, 82) tells you in what year the article was abstracted. A complete citation is given at the beginning of the abstract.

Whenever you locate an abstract that seems useful, take a few minutes to notice what other research is classified under the same heading in *Sociological Abstracts*. Sometimes you may miss useful materials because you fail to locate them in the index. Becoming familiar with how abstracts are organized topically gives you an alternative way to search for relevant research.

Although *Sociological Abstracts* is probably most helpful to sociology students, specialized abstracts are available for other social science disciplines. Anthropological research is abstracted in *Abstracts in Anthropology,* psychological research is abstracted in *Psychological Abstracts,* and economic and political science research is indexed in the *Public Affairs Information Service (PAIS) Bulletin.*

Dissertation Abstracts International (DAI)

The abstracts of doctoral dissertations are published twelve times each year in one of two sets of *DAI*. Social sciences and humanities dissertations appear in issues marked "A," natural science and psychology dissertations in issues marked "B." As in *Social Sciences Citation Index,* entries in *Dissertation Abstracts International* are arranged in broad categories and also indexed by key words from the titles of the dissertations. A wide variety of research may be represented by a single category label, but dissertation title and area of specialization will help you identify potentially helpful research.

Under the heading "Retirement," excerpted from the index for *DAI* shown here (Figure 7), is listed a thesis on retirement communities in Japan. The number that follows the title indicates that the thesis is abstracted on page 3718 of Part A of *DAI* (Figure 8). On that page, in addition to the abstract itself, the institution where the thesis was submitted, the date when it was published, and its length are given. The chair of the student's thesis committee is often listed as well.

You should probably explore the other indexes and abstracts I have mentioned before settling down in front of *Dissertation Abstracts International.* Although they often provide an up-to-date re-

RETIREMENT

RETIREMENT
PRE-RETIREMENT NEEDS OF SUBURBAN PUBLIC
    SCHOOL EDUCATORS (PLANNING, RETIREMENT,
    ATTITUDE, PREPARATION, PROFESSIONAL PERSONNEL,
    ADJUSTMENT) (EDUCATION, ADMINISTRATION)
    BURKE, RALPH MCDERMOTT, JR., p.3490–A
SOCIAL INTEGRATION AT A JAPANESE RETIREMENT
    COMMUNITY (GERONTOLOGY) KINOSHITA,
    YASUHITO, p.3718–A

Figure 7.   Excerpt from *DAI*.

view of the literature in a particular field, obtaining dissertations can be both costly and time-consuming. Universities that contribute to *DAI* do not lend the original dissertation, relying instead on University Microfilms International to sell microfilm copies (or, at a premium price, paper reproductions) to libraries and researchers. Although some copies of dissertations that have been purchased by libraries are available through interlibrary loan, in most cases you will have to purchase the copy directly from University Microfilms International, a Bell & Howell subsidiary. If you are working on a long-term project and after reading its abstract you feel that a dissertation would be extremely helpful, it may be worth the time and expense to order it. Otherwise, you can expect much thesis research to appear in following years in other forms as young scholars revise their work for publication in journals and books.

Nearly all important indexes and abstracts are now available as online computer data bases, and most college libraries offer searching services of some kind. Computer searching can cover vast quantities of citations in seconds. Data bases can also be searched using combinations of terms not possible in printed products. Your librarian can advise you as to the appropriateness of a computer search on your topic.

THE LIBRARY'S CATALOG

Research appearing in journals will probably constitute the bulk of references you use in any type of social science writing but, in addition to these, you will want to explore other formats used to report research. Books are the logical next place to look. If

SOCIAL INTEGRATION AT A JAPANESE RETIREMENT
COMMUNITY   Order No. DA8503732

KINOSHITA, YASUHITO, PH.D. *University of California, San Francisco,* 1984. 349pp. Chairman: Christie W. Kiefer

This dissertation is an ethnographic study of social behavior among the residents in a planned retirement community in Japan. It explores the issue of social integration within the overall theoretical framework of Social Interactionism and the emic perspective of Japanese culture.

It is based on 13 months of field work, during which I lived in this community. Participant observation, interviewing, and unobtrusive measures constitute the methodology, although the data for this dissertation are primarily observational.

The dissertation has three parts. Part One provides an overview of Japanese aging, which includes demographic characteristics, the impact of social change, the current welfare system for the aged, and the current state of development of retirement communities. In short, the socio-cultural background for the emergence of retirement communities is discussed.

Part Two is concerned with the description of the research setting and the demographic characteristics of the residents. Overall, the residents represent an elite segment of their generation, and have similar socio-economic backgrounds.

Social integration is discussed in Part Three. Major problems between the management and the residents are analyzed with regard to the unique cultural meanings of "contract," "welfare," and "contract welfare." The role and functions of the Residents Association as a formal organization and those of various groups and individual informal activities are presented. This discussion centers on types of roles and their availability, and on the relationship between roles and social integration. Patterns of social interaction are discussed with regard to activity in the community, key behavioral norms, the management of interactional distance, socialization, and friendship.

I conclude that the insulation of the elderly itself does not promote social integration in this setting. Rather, new roles must emerge that will help the residents structure a newly constituted, informal, and unstructured social situation. This is further discussed in the context of Japanese culture.

Figure 8.   Excerpt from *DAI.*

you know of an expert on your topic, you can go directly to the author's name to see whether your library has any books written by this scholar. Otherwise, your efforts are best spent searching for any materials housed in your library that pertain to your specific subject. To do this effectively, you need to know something about the subject headings used by libraries to bring together related books.

Most libraries use the Library of Congress subject headings. The first step, then, is to make sure that you search for your topic using the appropriate vocabulary. A convenient way to do this is to consult *Subject Headings Used in the Dictionary Catalogs of the Library of Congress*. (If your library uses the Dewey Decimal System, however, consult *Sears List of Subject Headings*.) If you searched for materials pertaining to retirement and retirement communities in the Library of Congress listing, you would find the headings shown in Figure 9.

Any word or phrase appearing in boldface type (e.g., *Retirement communities*) is a heading that may be used in the catalog. Indented below a heading and prefixed by "sa" (the abbreviation for "see also") are other headings used in the catalog. (In this example, you are advised to see also "Life care communities.") A word or phrase preceded by an "x" is *not* used in the catalog; information on these topics (e.g., "Places of retirement") are found instead under the boldface heading that comes before these phrases ("Retirement, Places of"). The "xx" prefix stands for "see also (from)." For example, under "Retirement, Mandatory," "Retirement age" is prefixed by "xx." Under the boldface heading "Retirement age," there is an "sa" reference to "Retirement, Mandatory." Words or phrases prefixed by a dash indicate a subheading of the major topic heading ("Retirement, Mandatory. Law and legislation.") Headings that appear in light-face type are not used in the catalog, but you are directed to see the proper heading (e.g., information on "Retirement pensions" is found under "Civil service pensions," "Old age pensions," and "Pensions").

Because "Retirement communities" is a recognized (boldface) heading in the Library of Congress list, you can find the heading in the catalog, and after it are listed all relevant books. The scope note under the phrase points out the distinction between retirement communities and life care communities.

Retirement, Mandatory   *(Indirect)*
  sa Retirement age
  x Mandatory retirement
  xx Retirement age
— Law and legislation   *(Indirect)*
    xx Labor laws and legislation
Retirement, Places of   *(Indirect)*
  sa Retirement communities
  x Places of retirement
Retirement accounts, Individual
    See Individual retirement accounts
Retirement age   *(Indirect)*   *(HD7105-7106)*
  sa Retirement, Mandatory
  x Age of retirement
    Pension age
  xx Age and employment
    Retirement, Mandatory
Retirement communities   *(Indirect)*
    Here are entered works on planned resi-
      dential developments designed for the
      aged. Works on planned residential de-
      velopments for the aged which also
      provide meal service, medical care,
      etc. are entered under Life care com-
      munities.
  sa Life care communities
  xx Aged—Dwellings
    Retirement, Places of
  Note under Life care communities
Retirement contributions as tax deductions
    See Income tax—Deductions—Retirement
      contributions
Retirement income   *(Indirect)*
  sa Old age pensions
  xx Aged
    Aged—Economic conditions
    Income
    Retirement
— Effect of inflation on
    xx Inflation (Finance)
Retirement pensions
    See Civil service pensions
    Old age pensions
    Pensions
Retirement test (Old age pensions)
    See Old age pensions—Retirement test

Figure 9.   Excerpt from *Subject Headings Used in
the Dictionary Catalogs of the Library of Congress.*

Many libraries still maintain a catalog consisting of large card files, but you might find that your library has replaced these with microfilm, microfiche, or direct-access computer terminals. In looking through the card catalog at my college library, I found the following entry (Figure 10):

```
HQ
1063      Jacobs, Jerry.
J3            Fun city : an ethnographic study of a
1983      retirement community / by Jerry Jacobs.
          -- Prospect Heights, Ill. : Waveland
          Press, 1983, c1974.
             viii, 87 p. ill. 23 cm.
          Bibliography: p. 86-87.
          ISBN 0-38133-024-8


             1. Retirement communities--United
          States--Case studies.  I. Title


MWelC   05 OCT 84              WELLat
```

Figure 10.   Library card.

To the left of the bibliographic information on this card is the library call number for Jerry Jacob's *Fun City:* HQ 1063 J3 1983. If your library has an open stack policy, spend some time poking around the HQ 1063 shelves for additional books that look interesting. In fact, if you continue to do library research in the social sciences, you will become quite familiar with the H section ("H" denotes social sciences) of the library collection. Second letters following H denote subfields of either economics (H-HJ) or sociology (HM-HX). Other books shelved under HQ, for example, deal with the family, marriage, and women. Economic theory and economic history are found under HB and HC; works on communities, class, and race are shelved under HT; and so forth. Political science is classified under J, and anthropology under GN.

GOVERNMENT PUBLICATIONS

Government reports are one source of information with which you may not have been familiar before taking courses in the social sciences. When you think about government publications, the decennial census probably comes to mind; but each year, the U.S. government publishes thousands of pages of documents covering topics ranging from the health hazards associated with smoking to the latest developments in farming technology. Many of these publications are regularly sent to libraries designated as "depositories" of federal documents. Most large university and some larger public libraries (as well as a few college libraries) are government depositories. Your reference librarian will be able to identify the one nearest you. Because the information produced by the U.S. Government Printing Office is quite voluminous, many of these documents may not be entered in the library's general catalog. You may instead need to rely on a printed catalog issued monthly by the U.S. government.

The *Monthly Catalog of U.S. Government Publications* provides information on documents produced by all three branches of the federal government within several months after they are published. Each issue of the catalog is indexed separately, and cumulative indexes are compiled annually, every five years, and every ten years. The index follows the format of the Library of Congress subject headings—a series of major headings subdivided by topic and area. The 1985 cumulative index to the *Monthly Catalog* lists several entries under the heading of "Retirement." Your particular interest in retirement communities leads you to focus on the one that reads:

Retirement communities—United States—Food service.

Participants are satisfied with mandatory meal programs in HUD projects: report/, 85-24927.

If you wished to pursue this report on federal food service projects among the elderly, you would look through the catalog for the entry numbered 85-24927. The prefix "85-" denotes the year the item was listed in the *Monthly Catalog;* the last five digits denote the sequential listing within the year. The entry you find appears in Figure 11.

The boldface number at the top of the description is the Superintendent of Documents classification number for the report. (Most depository libraries shelve documents apart from their regular holdings; if your library has a documents collection, you

85-24927

GA 1.13:RCED-85-67

United States. General Accounting Office.

Participants are satisfied with mandatory meal programs in HUD projects : report / by the U.S. General Accounting Office. — Washington, D.C. : The Office, [1985]

8, 36 p. : ill. ; 28 cm. Cover title. Distributed to depository libraries in microfiche. "March 5, 1985." "GAO/RCED-85-67." "B-217752"—p. [1] (1st group). ●Item 546-D (microfiche)

1. Aged — United States — Dwellings. 2. Retirement communities — United States — Food service. 3. Aged — United States — Nutrition. 4. United States. Dept. of Housing and Urban Development. I. Title. OCLC 11962633

Figure 11.   Excerpt from the *Monthly Catalog*.

should be able to find it under the GA 1.13 section of that collection.) The first line following the classification number gives the author of the document (e.g., the General Accounting Office). The description that follows does not provide you with any additional substantive information about the report, although it does tell you its length (38 pages), that it was distributed to depository libraries in microfiche, and what subject headings were assigned to it. If your library does not possess a copy of this report, your librarian can advise you how to go about getting one.

The *Monthly Catalog* is only one way to search for materials published by the federal government. Other, more specialized, guides to locating government publications are prepared by some departments of the government (e.g., the U.S. Bureau of the Census—a division of the Department of Commerce—publishes a catalog of census publications, and the U.S. Bureau of Labor Statistics—a division of the Department of Labor—publishes a guide to labor statistics). *American Statistics Index* is a commercially published special index designed to help you identify the subject matter of statistical tables in government publications. It requires both experience and patience and, often, the assistance of a librarian, to find your way through the wealth of publications that accumulate in your library's documents section, but don't ignore them when writing research papers. They can provide valuable contextual information as well as primary data.

"BUT THE LIBRARY DOESN'T HAVE IT": USING LIBRARY NETWORKS

For several reasons your library may not have the books, journal articles, or government publications you want. The first reason is expense. Journal subscriptions, in particular, are costly, and your library may be able to collect only the major research journals in each academic discipline. Journals that have a highly limited audience (e.g., gerontologists, demographers, or specialists in family violence) are likely to be found only in university libraries associated with specialized graduate programs. Furthermore, even if your library currently subscribes to a journal on your list, the library may not have the issue you need. There may be gaps in the library's holdings, or your library may have only recently begun to subscribe to a journal of which you need an older issue. Similarly, you cannot expect your library, no matter how large it is, to receive all of the books or government reports published each year.

Just because your library does not have what you are looking for does not mean that you must scratch a reference from your list. Because libraries are linked in a network of reciprocal borrowing, it is not necessary for each library to have everything. Many college libraries belong to local lending consortiums that allow students at one institution to use the library at another. If materials are not available locally, your library can probably get them from another library through the broader, interlibrary loan network. But as I mentioned earlier, all of these arrangements take time. You will have to travel to another library with which you may not be familiar, or wait days or even weeks to receive a book or a copy of an article through interlibrary loan. The implied message is not to give up, but to begin your library search as soon as possible.

A FINAL COMMENT: FAMILIAR TERRAIN

Regardless of the discipline, there is some degree of consensus among scholars about the major journals in their fields. There is much argument, to be sure, as to whether the research published in these journals represents the best work of these disciplines, but there is usually little doubt that scholars are at least looking at, if not reading, what is being published in these journals. Another way in which major journals may be defined is through library subscriptions; these are the journals you can expect to find in even the smallest research libraries.

Listed here are some of the major journals read by social scientists. I have included them here to give you some means of evaluating the materials you locate. An article appearing in one of these journals has been granted a certain legitimacy by its respective discipline. Several of these journals are the "official publication" of the major professional association of a discipline—for example, the American Sociological Association. These journals are also read by a broad audience. As you explore a particular topic, you will become familiar with many other journals that report research on specialized topics (e.g., *Research on Aging, Gerontology, The Gerontologist*).

ANTHROPOLOGY

American Anthropologist

American Antiquity

American Ethnologist

Anthropological Quarterly

Current Anthropology

Journal of Anthropological Research

Man

ECONOMICS

American Economic Review

Journal of Economic Literature (which includes a bibliography of
   current articles in each issue)

Journal of Political Economy

Review of Economics and Statistics

POLITICAL SCIENCE

American Journal of Political Science
American Political Science Review
Foreign Affairs
Foreign Policy
Journal of Politics
Political Science Quarterly

PSYCHOLOGY

American Psychologist
Contemporary Psychology (a journal of reviews)
Developmental Psychology
Psychological Bulletin
Psychological Review
Journal of Personality and Social Psychology

SOCIOLOGY

American Sociological Review
American Journal of Sociology
Social Forces
Social Problems
Contemporary Sociology (a journal of reviews)
Annual Review of Sociology

7

Form

Form refers to what your paper looks like: Is it typed double spaced? Are the margins adequate? Are the quotation marks in the right place? Are sources properly acknowledged? Following proper form does more than make your paper look nice. It makes a difference in how others read your work; a messy paper distracts readers from the point you are trying to make. Failing to follow proper form may even determine whether your paper is read at all. Many journals return manuscripts to authors who do not follow the guidelines for submissions, and instructors may refuse to accept papers that they judge too difficult to read. More important, form can affect the content of your writing. Misplaced quotation marks or failure to acknowledge sources can result in plagiarism.

The accepted forms in sociology, psychology, and social psychology, for example, differ from each other; even within any *one* of these disciplines, forms differ in various journals. The material in this chapter outlines one approach to addressing questions of form that arise in social science writing. Regardless of whether you follow this or another set of guidelines, the most important factor in manuscript form is *consistency*. Make certain that citations to works by a single author follow the same pattern, that footnotes are consistent in style, and so forth. Consistency of form will help your reader focus on what you have written, not on how it appears on the page.

MANUSCRIPT FORM

Most people assume they know how to put a paper together before they hand it in. At the risk of insulting your intelligence, here are some guidelines for preparing the last draft of a manuscript:

1. Type your manuscript on 8½ × 11-inch paper. Use conventional typing paper; avoid the variety of exotic papers—onion skin, colored, lined, scented, spiral-bound, bordered, or whatnot—found on the shelves of campus bookstores. (And do not use erasable typing paper. Although it makes typing easier, the ink tends to come off the paper and stick to a reader's hand.) If you type your paper on a word processor and print it on continuous feed paper, remove the perforated edges, separate the pages, and arrange them in order.

2. Type, double-spacing, on one side of the paper only. Make sure your final copy is dark enough to be easily read.

3. If your paper is fairly long (ten pages or more), include a title page. Center your title about midway down the page. Roughly 1 inch from the bottom, center your name, the course number or name, and the date. If the title is longer than one line, double space it. Single space the information about authorship.

If you do not use a title page, place your name, course title, and date in the upper right-hand corner of the page (single spaced), about one inch from the top. Skip two lines and center your title, double spacing between lines for long titles. Leave three or four lines before starting your paper.

4. Capitalize the first and last words of your title, as well as all other words except articles, conjunctions, and prepositions. Do not place the title in quotation marks or underline it. If, however, the title contains the name of a book, the book title should be underlined, for example,

An Analysis of the Loss of Community in Erikson's

Everything in Its Path

5. Provide ample and uniform margins for your paper. Allow 1½ inches for the left side margin and 1 inch for the

right, bottom, and top margins. Annotations are easier to make and to read with generous margins.

6. Number the pages consecutively. If you use a title page, don't number it. The first page of your paper needn't be numbered either, but number each subsequent page (beginning with 2) in the same place, either in the upper right-hand corner or centered at the bottom of the page. Do *not* put a period after the number. Place your last name in the upper right-hand corner of each page, and skip two lines before beginning the text. Pages with notes and references should be numbered as text, but you need not number pages with tables or appendixes attached to the end of the paper.

7. Indent a uniform number of spaces—either five or eight— at the beginning of each paragraph. Direct quotations longer than four lines should be indented (also five or eight spaces) and typed single spaced (see the next section on "Quotations and Quotation Marks").

8. Make a photocopy of your paper before you hand it in. Your instructor probably shares your fear of losing a paper.

9. Staple your paper in the upper left-hand corner; paper clips can become attached to other student papers. If your paper is too long for a standard staple, use some sort of heavy clip to hold it together. Avoid those clear plastic binders that can cause an avalanche of student papers on an instructor's desk. And avoid stiff folders that add bulk to an instructor's load.

QUOTATIONS AND QUOTATION MARKS

Both quotations and quotation marks are powerful writing devices when used sparingly. They signal your reader to pay close attention to what is being said. When overused, however, they can have the opposite effect, prompting your reader to skim through the quoted material in search of the point you are trying to make. You are *writing* a paper, not compiling an anthology. For each quotation you consider including in your paper, ask the following questions:

Can I write a valid and concise summary or paraphrase of these words? If you can accurately convey the meaning of the quoted material, you should probably summarize or paraphrase it and properly acknowledge the source (see the next section on citation form). A summary is a condensation of the original; a paraphrase ("putting it in your own words") can be as long as the original or even longer. You don't want to swamp your paper with long quotations, so, for balance, you summarize. Papers composed of an endless stream of direct quotations not only are boring to read, but they fail to demonstrate an understanding of the source materials themselves. You also don't want to jar your reader by even a short quotation of someone else's distinctive voice (unless it is that distinctive voice you want to introduce), so you paraphrase.

Sometimes a summary won't do: it would take more words or an awkward construction to capture the essence of the quotation (e.g., the author's choice of words cannot be improved on), or the quotation is to be used as evidence for a point you will make (e.g., interviews from a field study). In these cases don't hesitate to quote directly; just be sure to keep track of the balance in your paper between your own words and those of others.

Caution: when you summarize or paraphrase, be sure to give credit to your source, even if you are putting the material entirely into your own words.

Do I need this quotation to make my point, and do I adequately explain why I am using this quotation? Make certain that you, as well as your readers, know why each quotation appears in your paper. The simplest way to accomplish this is to introduce and follow the quotation with some discussion of it. The language you use to introduce the quoted material should do more than state the source; it should convey a sense of your purpose in including the material in your paper. Instead of writing, "Goffman says, . . . ," you might write, "Goffman claims, . . ." or "Goffman, on the other hand, concludes, . . ." or even "With customary eloquence, Goffman analyzes the dilemma that accompanies a shift in virtual and actual identities: . . . ." Instead of writing "Two respondents said: . . . ," you might write, "Placed side-by-side, the remarks of these two respondents illustrate the differences in motivation among group members: . . . ." Your discussion of quoted material, as well as the material itself, should be purposive rather than declaratory.

Is this a special case? Quotation marks are sometimes used to call attention to a concept or phrase of particular attribution. Many social science concepts are associated with their creators: Toennies's "Gemeinschaft" and "Gesellschaft," Cooley's "looking-glass self," Gans's "urban villagers," and Reisman's "other-directedness" come to mind. When we enclose these words in quotation marks, we are telling our readers that we have borrowed them and intended them to have the meaning given them by their originators. Because your paper can easily become cluttered with quotation marks, you might consider placing quotation marks only around the first occurrence (or underlining it), and omit identifying marks from later references to the phrase.

Once you decide which quotations to include in your paper, use an appropriate form to incorporate them. These rules can serve as guidelines:

1. Always identify the source of the quotation. Your reader should never have to guess who or what the source of quoted material was. If you are quoting library materials, cite the author, year of publication, and page on which the material appears—for instance (Jones, 1985:227), (Bureau of the Census, 1981). (See "Citations Within the Text," page 123.) If you are quoting interviews you have conducted, give appropriate identifying information in parentheses after the quotation, for example (female, 42, office manager).

2. Distinguish between short and long quotations. If a quotation is four typewritten lines or less, incorporate it (double spaced) into the text. For example:

```
In commenting on the role of secrecy in bureaucracy, Weber

observes that "bureaucratic administration always tends

to be an administration of 'secret sessions': insofar as

it can, it hides its knowledge and action from criticism"

(Gerth and Mills, 1976:233).
```

Quotations longer than four typewritten lines should be indented, single spaced, and set off from the text by two blank lines. Do not place quotation marks around the material that is thus set off.

> The tendency toward secrecy in certain administrative
> fields follows their material nature: everywhere that the
> power interests of the domination structure toward the
> <u>outside</u> are at stake, whether it is an economic competitor
> of a private enterprise, or a foreign, potentially hos-
> tile polity, we find secrecy (Gerth and Mills, 1976:233).

3. Quote materials exactly. Anything placed within quotation marks should be the exact words found in the source. Do not alter verb tense, subject–verb agreement, or anything else about the quotation to make it fit into your text. Instead, change your text to conform to the quotation.

Similarly, retain the original punctuation and emphasis when quoting materials. In the first quotation from Weber, the phrase "secret sessions" appears in quotation marks in the source. Thus, the quotation marks are retained in the text, but as single, rather than double, quotes. (Single quotation marks are normally used for quotes within a quote.) In the second quotation, because the phrase "the outside" appears in italics in the original text, it is underlined in the quotation. If this phrase had not been emphasized in the source, but I wanted to draw attention to it myself, I would have appended the words "emphasis mine" to the parenthetic citation (e.g., Gerth and Mills, 1976:233, emphasis mine).

Sometimes quoted material contains mistakes of one kind or another: an awkward phrase or construction or a factual error. Such mistakes are common in direct transcriptions of interviews, where respondents may say one thing early in the interview and later contradict themselves. In such cases, attribute the odd phrase or expression to the source by placing the word *"sic"* after it in parentheses. This way your reader won't think your paper contains a misprint or typographical error. For instance, you may use a quotation in which a respondent says that he moved to Boston in 1977. In another quotation you want to include from the same interview, this man says "In 1979 *(sic)*, when we first came to Boston . . . ," you note the change of date by placing *sic* immediately after 1979.

Finally, if you must alter the original quotation to include it properly in the text, identify any words you *add* by placing them in brackets, not parentheses, inside of the quotation marks; indicate *omission* of any words by ellipses (three periods). While researching a book on Alaska, I came across the following text from a report issued by the Alaska Statehood Commission:

> The overwhelming majority of Alaskans, including all members of this commission, consider themselves Americans. We remember with deep gratitude the spring of 1964, when money and equipment and manpower came from across America to rebuild our earthquake crumpled coastal cities. That support drew on vast stores of supplies and equipment that an independent Alaska could never provide. We are proud to be citizens of a nation which responded so generously, and want to pass this citizenship to our descendants (Alaska Statehood Commission, 1982:40).

To shorten the quotation yet preserve its meaning, I arrived at this revision (note that the ellipsis is followed by a fourth period because it ends a sentence):

```
The overwhelming majority of Alaskans, including all
members of this commission, consider themselves Ameri-
cans. . . . We are proud to be citizens of a nation which
responded so generously [to the devastation wrought by
the earthquake of 1964], and want to pass this citizen-
ship to our descendants (Alaska Statehood Commission,
1982:40).
```

CITATIONS WITHIN THE TEXT

Unlike writers in the humanities, who follow the guidelines established by the Modern Language Association, social science authors do not have a standard format for citing reference works. Many social science disciplines have begun to adopt citation formats similar to the one established by the American Psychological Association (*Publication Manual of the American Psychological Association,* 1983), but the major journals in most social science fields still fail to offer consistent advice. The rules outlined in this section indicate one possible way of placing citations within the text; check with your instructor (or a specific journal's style sheet) to make sure you choose the appropriate form.

Citations to source material, regardless of whether you paraphrase or quote directly, are made within the text, not within footnotes. The citations provide enough information so that your reader can find the complete reference for the source material at the end of your paper, in the References or Bibliography section.

The specific form of text citations varies slightly, depending on what is being cited, but the following general rules apply to all text citations:

1. When the author's name is not mentioned in the text, it should be included in the citation, along with the date of publication, and sometimes the page number. All of this information is placed in parentheses directly after the cited material; the author's name is followed by a comma, and the date of publication is followed by a colon when a page number is included. Page numbers should be given only if the cited material is quoted directly.

    The image of the frontier evolved out of the "paired but contradictory ideas of nature and civilization" (Smith, 1954:305).

    These results support the information hypothesis (Ritchey, 1976), which argues that migrants learn of economic opportunities from established residents.

Notice that the authors, Smith in the first example and Ritchey in the second, are named within the parenthetic citation, because they are not named in the paper's text. Notice, as well, that the citation is placed outside of the quotation marks and the period that ends the sentence appears *after* the closing parenthesis.

2. When an author is mentioned in the text, the name is not repeated in the citation, but the date (and, if directly quoted, the page number) is given in parentheses after the author's name.

    Goldman and Dickens (1983:585) define the "commodification of the rural myth" as the "packaging of the images and

value system of rural life as if they are contained in the
commodity with which they are being associated."

3. When repeated citations to the same reference are made,
give the date and page number (if appropriate) for the first citation;
for later citations list only the page number. This rule is appropriate
when the subject of your paper is a detailed analysis of one or two
texts. Because it should be obvious to the reader that you are repeatedly quoting the same source, the date of publication is super-
fluous.

The assumptions implicit in Karl Marx's later writing are
found in his Economic and Philosophical Manuscripts of
1844 (1961). It is there, for example, that we find the
clearest outline of his conceptions regarding human nature. Marx (36) writes: . . . .

If, however, you make repeated references to several works
by one author, you must provide complete citations (including
both year of publication and page number) for each work, following the form previously described in rules 1 and 2.

4. For serial citations (i.e., when several sources provide evidence for the same argument), list the authors in alphabetical order, and separate the citations with semicolons. Enclose the multiple citations in parentheses.

Friends and family members may encourage migration by
providing information about economic opportunities or
social conditions elsewhere (Bieder, 1973; Brown et al.,
1963; Choldin, 1973; Litwak, 1960).

5. When a source has two authors, include both last names in
the citation. When a source has three or more authors, follow the

first author's name with *et al.* (the Latin abbreviation for *et alii*, meaning "and other people"). The References section, however, includes the last names of all authors for a given source. The examples in rules 2 and 4 illustrate how to cite works of joint authorship.

6. When you include two or more works written by the same person in the same year, designate them "a," "b," and so forth. Usually, citations are labeled in the order in which they appear in the text—for example, the first appearance is "a," the second is "b."

> Gove (1970a,b) has been one of the most outspoken critics
>
> of labeling theory.

7. When two or more authors have the same last name, identify each in the text by the appropriate initials.

> Evidence that both confirms (R. J. Smith, 1983) and dis-
>
> putes (J. K. Smith, 1984) this hypothesis has been uncov-
>
> ered.

THE LIST OF WORKS CITED

The References section of your paper elaborates on the text citations by giving the complete names of authors, places of publication, publishers, and page numbers. Every text citation must be included in the References; any materials not cited in the text are usually omitted from the References. The format for entries is determined by the type of research material.

Books with a Single Author

References to books include the author's name (last name first), the date of publication, the title of the book, the place of publication, and the publisher (in this order).

```
Gans, Herbert J. 1962. The Urban Villagers. New York:
    Free Press.
Nash, Roderick. 1967. Wilderness and the American
    Mind. New Haven: Yale University Press.
```

The author's last name, flush against the left margin, is followed by a comma, the first name, and a period. (If a middle initial is used, a second period is not appended.) A period is also placed after the date of publication. The title, underlined continuously, ends with a period. Subtitles are commonly omitted from the References. The place of publication is usually given by town or city name only, but state names are included if a place is not widely known, or if the place (e.g., Cambridge, Massachusetts) can be confused with another place (Cambridge, England). Place of publication is followed by a colon and ends with the name of the publisher.

Note that the second (and any additional) line in the reference is indented. The references should also be typed double spaced.

Books with More than One Author

If a book has two authors, list it alphabetically by the last name of the first author. A comma follows the first author, and the second author's name is listed in normal order—first name first.

```
Arrington, Leonard J., and Davis Bitton. 1979. The
    Mormon Experience. New York: Knopf.
```

If a book has more than two authors, list it alphabetically by the last name of the first author, then list the names of all of the remaining authors in normal order as they appear on the title page.

```
Kresge, David T., Thomas A Morehouse, and George W.
    Rogers. 1977. Issues in Alaska Development. Seat-
    tle: University of Washington Press.
```

Government Documents

Unless an author appears on the report, list the government agency as the author of the document.

```
U.S. Bureau of the Census. 1978. Estimates of the Pop-
    ulation of Counties and Metropolitan Areas: July 1,
    1977 and 1978. Washington D.C.: Government Print-
    ing Office.
```

Works of Corporate Authorship

Sometimes cities, consulting firms, research agencies, or other corporate bodies issue reports on which no author is named. If no publisher is named, assume the corporate body is the publisher.

```
Anchorage Resource Information Service. 1978. Anchor-
    age Quarterly: A Review of Socio-Economic Data,
    Vol. 1, no. 1. Anchorage: Anchorage Resource Infor-
    mation Service.
```

An Edited Book

If you cite a book with an editor but no author (e.g., an edited collection of papers written by others), begin the citation with the editor's last name.

```
Smith, Valene L., ed. 1977. Hosts and Guests. Philadel-
    phia: University of Pennsylvania Press.
```

A Translated Book

Unless you are discussing the translation itself—for instance, comparing one translation of a work with another—list the book by its author, not by its translator.

```
Khazanov, A. M. 1984. Nomads and the Outside World.
    Translated by Julia Crookenden. New York: Cam-
    bridge University Press.
```

An Article in an Edited Collection

If you cite a single article in an edited volume of several articles, list the work by the author of the article, not the editor.

Bardo, John W., and Deborah J. Bardo. 1980. "From Settlers to Migrants: A Symbolic Interpretation of American Migration to Australia." Pp. 193–232 in Studies in Symbolic Interaction, Vol. 1, edited by Norman K. Denzin. Greenwich, Conn.: JAI Press.

An Article in a Scholarly Journal

Place the title of the article in quotation marks; underline the title of the journal. Do not abbreviate either title. Give the volume and page numbers, separated by a colon, at the end of the entry.

Fischer, Claude S. 1975. "Toward a Subcultural Theory of Urbanism." American Journal of Sociology 80:1319–1341.

An Article in a Popular Magazine

List the article by the author's last name, or if no author is given for the article, list it by the title of the article, or by the second word if the first word is "A," "An," or "The." Thus, an anonymous article called "The American Way of Life" would be listed alphabetically under "American," even though the citation would retain the "The" of the title.

Johnson, Robert S. "Making Big Business Pay." U.S. News and World Report (22 July 1977):32–33.

"The Making of a Superstar." Newsweek (19 March 1983): 23–25.

An Article in a Newspaper

The only difference between references for a magazine and those for a newspaper is the inclusion of a section number with a newspaper reference. If the newspaper is not divided into sections, the format is exactly the same.

Martinson, Jacob. "The Psychology of Selflessness." New York Times (15 April 1968), sec. 3:5–6.

Multiple Citations for a Single Author

If you cite several works written by the same person, arrange them alphabetically by title and precede the second and all subsequent entries with eight underlined spaces and a period.

> Morrison, Peter A. 1971. "Chronic Movers and the Future Redistribution of Population: A Longitudinal Analysis." Demography 8:171–184.
>
> _____. 1967. "Duration of Residence and Prospective Migration: The Evaluation of a Stochastic Model." Demography 4:553–561.

Combining Entries in a References Section: An Illustration

When you have compiled the relevant information for works to be included in your References section, arrange them alphabetically by the author's last name. Type the entries on a separate page titled "References," double-spacing each entry and double-spacing between each entry. Begin the first line of each entry against the left-hand margin, and indent all remaining lines of the entry five to eight spaces. Underline the titles of all books, reports, government documents, journals, magazines, and newspapers.

Here is an illustration of the first page of a References section:

References

Alaska Statehood Commission. 1982. More Perfect Union: A Preliminary Report of the Alaska Statehood Commission. Juneau: Alaska Statehood Commission.

Barnet, Sylvan, and Marcia Stubbs. 1986. Barnet and Stubbs's Practical Guide to Writing. Boston: Little, Brown and Company.

Becker, Howard S. 1963. Outsiders: Studies in the Sociology of Deviance. New York: The Free Press.

_____ 1986. Writing for Social Scientists. Chicago: University of Chicago Press.

Cuba, Lee J. 1984. "Reorientations of Self: Residential Identification in Anchorage, Alaska." Pp. 219–237 in Studies in Symbolic Interaction, Vol. 5, edited by Norman K. Denzin. Greenwich, Conn.: JAI Press.

```
Gerth, H. H., and C. Wright Mills, eds. 1976. From Max
    Weber: Essays in Sociology. New York: Oxford Univer-
    sity Press.
```

This example contains the first six entries in the References appearing in the back of this book. In comparing the two bibliographies, note that words italicized in print are underlined in typewritten papers.

NOTES

The use of notes in the text is governed by a simple rule: if possible, avoid them. This rule is based on the assumption that if an idea is important enough to include in a paper, it can (and should) be incorporated into the text. For the professional social scientist, the practice of avoiding notes whenever possible is also encouraged by editors who point to the cost of printing notes. There are, nevertheless, times when notes are an appropriate and important part of social science writing. In general, notes are necessary only when you are writing longer (ten pages or more) social science papers.

Possible Uses of Notes

1. Notes can provide detailed information that would otherwise detract from the narrative flow of the text. A note of this type is often used to elaborate on a research methodology. For example, you might write that "the interview schedule contained several questions designed to measure a respondent's tolerance for residential integration," and append a footnote describing the exact questions that were asked. If, however, you are planning to attach the interview schedule to the paper as an appendix, you would be better off drawing your reader's attention to this appendix with a parenthetical remark in the text, such as (see Appendix II), rather than using a note.

2. Notes can supply additional or analogous examples of a point raised in the text. Suppose you were writing about how people recognize and respond to strangers in urban neighborhoods. You might focus on how trust is established and maintained in

neighborhoods of this sort, but then speculate about the importance of trust in other settings in modern life (e.g., in buyer–seller relationships, in negotiations between corporations, or in author–publisher transactions). If an extended discussion of the importance of trust in modern society is not a major goal of your paper, a footnote might allow you to make this broader point without going too far afield of your thesis.

Do not use notes to supply additional citations for an issue raised in the text. Incorporate all of the relevant citations into the text using the form described earlier in this chapter.

3. Notes can anticipate questions or arguments that your readers might raise. When you write, you make decisions about how to organize your paper, what library materials to include, which tables to include, which explanation to offer for a particular finding, and so forth. Your reader, of course, cannot know how you arrived at all of these decisions, and, at times, you may feel that some sort of explanation is necessary. A note of this type may anticipate and argue against counterarguments (e.g., "You might be thinking that X, rather than Y, accounted for this finding, but let me tell you why that cannot be the case. . ."). Or it might explain why something that might be expected in the text is not there (e.g., "Sex and race were included in previous analyses, but neither of these variables exerted significant, independent effects on the dependent variable."). As with all other notes, use these sparingly. Your paper should not read like a "point–counterpoint" debate.

The Format for Notes

Two types of notes are commonly used: footnotes, which appear at the bottom of the appropriate page of text, and endnotes, which are collected and placed at the end of the paper. If you are using a typewriter, endnotes are easier to write, but the variety of text-editing software available makes footnotes equally painless if you are writing on a computer. If you use endnotes, type them, double spaced, on a separate page titled "Notes," and place them immediately after your text. Paginate the notes as though they were additional pages of text (e.g., if your text ends on page 22, the first page of notes is numbered 23). References (paginated), appendixes, and tables (both unpaginated) are placed after the notes.

Both footnotes and endnotes are inserted into the text in the same way. They are numbered consecutively throughout the paper; the numbers (*without* a period) are usually placed at the end of a sentence. The number of the note is either a superscript (placed one-half space above the line of text) or enclosed by brackets immediately following the sentence or phrase being noted.

```
The remainder of our observations yielded anticipated and
consistent results. 1
```

```
The remainder of our observations yielded anticipated and
consistent results. [1]
```

AVOIDING PLAGIARISM

Scholarship is an enterprise founded on trust. Although social science research is designed so that it can be replicated by others, the results of research studies are seldom verified. Because of the time and effort such verification would require, we must assume that both the data *and* their interpretation are the honest work of the author of the research. Without these assumptions, scholarly work would have little value or integrity. That is why the organizations that regulate academic life—universities and professional associations—reserve their harshest penalties for those who fabricate research findings or appropriate the words and ideas of others.

When you present the words or ideas of another as if they were your own, you are plagiarizing. When you quote directly or summarize in your own words the ideas of someone else, you must acknowledge your debts. You do so by making proper citations to source materials following a format such as that described earlier.

As easy as it might seem, claiming the work of others as your own is difficult to get away with. Professors who read student papers or referees who read papers for professional journals are intimately familiar with the published work in their disciplines; acquiring an in-depth knowledge of previous research is a major part of their graduate education. They can usually recognize if what they are reading has appeared someplace else. But more telling from the standpoint of student papers, professors know what to expect from their students. They do not expect undergraduate students to write papers of the quality published in scholarly journals. Their suspicions are likely to be aroused if they read a paper that appears professional in style or content.

Having been forewarned about the seriousness of plagiarism, how can you make sure no one ever accuses you of it? You can guard against unintentional plagiarism by providing unambiguous citations for either direct quotations or summaries of source materials. An example should help to illustrate. Assume that in the process of doing research for a paper on societal responses to deviant behavior, you come across the following conclusion by John Kitsuse:

> In modern society, the differentiation of deviants from the nondeviant population is increasingly contingent upon circumstances of situation, place, social and personal biography, and the bureaucratically organized activities and agencies of control (Kitsuse, 1962:256).

One way of incorporating this conclusion into your paper is to quote it in its entirety, acknowledging the source as I have done here. Another approach is to retain some of Kitsuse's words, embedded in the context of your own sentence. For example:

> As a proponent of labeling theory, Kitsuse (1962:256) argues that who and what is defined as deviant has more to do with "circumstances of situation, place, social and personal biography, and the bureaucratically organized activities and agencies of control" than with the behavior itself.

A third way to use Kitsuse's observation is to paraphrase it using your own words. A good paraphrase does not attempt to follow the same sentence structure or word choice as that of the source material. Instead, it conveys the gist of the original material

while presenting the ideas in another voice. An acceptable paraphrase of Kitsuse's material might read something like this (note
that because I am not using direct quotation, I have omitted the
reference to the page number):

> Labeling theorists have concluded that who and what are
> defined as deviant is determined by a host of factors that
> have little to do with behavior itself—where and when
> the act is committed, who is committing it, and who is re-
> sponding to it (Kitsuse, 1962).

Compare this with a bad paraphrase of the same material:

> In contemporary society, distinguishing deviants from
> non-deviants is more and more determined by characteris-
> tics of context, location, societal and individual biog-
> raphy, and the bureaucratic organization and agencies of
> social control (Kitsuse, 1962:256).

Here the writer has merely provided synonyms—"contemporary society" for Kitsuse's "modern society," for example.
There is no point to this paraphrase. Verbatim quotation of the
original sentence is much to be preferred over this mechanical,
word-for-word substitution.

In attempting to avoid plagiarism, students sometimes give
credit where it is not necessarily due. Some material unearthed by
your library research can justifiably be labeled "common knowledge"—information about a topic that requires no citation to a
particular source. What qualifies as common knowledge? Anything
that is repeatedly mentioned in published materials but never cited
is probably fair game, for example, that Spanish is the native language of most immigrants from Cuba. Definitions from standard
dictionaries (not specialized dictionaries, like those mentioned in
Chapter 6) do not require acknowledgment, but neither are they

likely to add much to your paper. Statements of historical fact (e.g., "The Oneida community was founded in 1848" or "Ronald Reagan was elected president in 1980") need not be acknowledged, barring some controversy over the date or location of a particular occurrence. On the other hand, interpretations of historical events must be properly acknowledged (e.g., "When the Oneida community was formed in 1848, a new era in utopian experiments began" or "The election of Ronald Reagan as president in 1980 signaled a dramatic shift in political opinion"). The more you read about a particular subject, the greater the chance you will be able to judge what passes as common knowledge. If in doubt, the obvious solution is to err on the side of caution by acknowledging the source.

AVOIDING SEXIST LANGUAGE

> The leader will not give orders that will not be obeyed. . . . If he must give orders when they are expected and will be obeyed, he must not give orders when they will not and cannot be obeyed. The leader must maintain his own position. His social rank is in mutual dependence with the authority of his orders. When he gives orders that are not obeyed, he has by that fact undermined his rank and hence the presumption on the part of the members of his group that his future orders are to be obeyed. Nothing, moreover, will create more confusion in the minds of his followers, and nothing so quickly lead them to doubt his confidence. (Homans, 1950:429)

When George Homans published *The Human Group* in 1950, perhaps few readers were put off by the style in which it was written. Today, however, many would be troubled by the abundance of masculine pronouns in Homans's book. Is he suggesting (in the passage quoted here) that all leaders are men and, therefore, that the repeated use of masculine pronouns is appropriate? Probably not. But Homans's style is nevertheless offensive because of its implicit sexism. It would be easy to rewrite this passage without using sexist language, at the same time retaining its original meaning. In your own writing, watch out for the unnecessary use of masculine pronouns.

Sexist language creates particular problems in social science writing, where gender plays a major role in explaining a variety of social phenomena. To describe leaders, deviants, or managers as men through the use of masculine pronouns is to imply either that men occupy the majority of these roles or that men and women lead, deviate, or manage in the same way. Neither of these scenarios may be accurate, and the use of sexist language only invites stylistic, as well as analytic, criticism.

How, then, do you avoid sexist language? Sometimes you can do without personal pronouns—masculine or feminine—altogether. Take, for example, the last sentence of the paragraph quoted previously. One possible revision would be the following:

```
Nothing, moreover, will create more confusion in the

minds of followers, and nothing so quickly move them to

doubt a leader's confidence.
```

In the original, "his" is used to describe "followers," but is this really necessary? To whom other than the leader could the followers belong? I have changed the second "his" to "leader's"; in using the possessive of the role itself, I am able to avoid gender-specific pronouns. (I have also replaced "lead them" with "move them" in order to avoid "lead them to doubt a leader's. . . .") In general, think twice before using personal pronouns in your writing; make sure they are important to what you have to say.

Another way to purge sexist language from your writing is to change "he" to "he and she" (or "she and he") and to replace "his" with "his or her" (or "her or his"). The obvious problem with these substitutions is that they clutter a sentence with tiresome repetitions. A writer can make one or two such replacements without much effect on his or her prose. But he or she may lose the patience of his or her reader if he or she attempts universally to replace "he" with "he or she." (The abbreviated forms "s/he" and "her/his" are not much better.)

The preferred solution is to use, where possible, a plural subject paired with the pronoun "their." To return to Homans, we might rewrite the second sentence of the quotation as follows:

```
If leaders must give orders when they are expected and

will be obeyed, they must not give orders when they will-

not and cannot be obeyed.
```

Using plurals is the most convenient way of avoiding sexist language. It also does not distort the meaning of statements that are intended to describe social interaction of both women and men.

One final note: avoid the sexist expressions "man" and "mankind" when referring to attributes or behavior characteristic of all humans. Instead of writing "It is man's nature to . . . ," write "It is human nature. . . ." Likewise, substitute "humanity" or "people" for "mankind" (e.g., "all of humanity" instead of "all of mankind").

8
Revising

In the first chapter, I revised a passage of my own writing. To illustrate the process of writing, I discussed the general benefits of rewriting and rethinking, but I didn't take the time to discuss in detail how to revise a paper. In this final chapter, I describe several types of revision—for content, for clarity, for conciseness, for proper word usage, for spelling, for grammar—that may help you identify weaknesses in your writing.

The examples in this chapter, clearly set off for examination, may give the appearance that revising is a simple task; it isn't. Sentences in need of repair do not jump from the page. You must go looking for them or ask others to help you find them. When you read a draft of a paper you have written, bear in mind the importance of objectifying your writing, distancing yourself from your writing and approaching it as an outsider. (In Chapter 1, I discussed some ways of accomplishing this.) Above all, allow time to put your draft aside, preferably for a day but at least for a few hours, so you can approach it with a relatively open mind, and allow plenty of time for revision. Editing and rewriting are as much a part of the writing process as committing your initial thoughts to paper.

Although revising requires a substantial investment of time and effort, you don't have to know a lot of grammar to be a good editor. If you are like most of us, you edit your writing, as Howard Becker (1986) puts it, "by ear." You pause at sentences that don't sound right, and try to come up with ways of making them sound better. It doesn't matter if you can't tell a comma fault from a dangling modifier, as long as you make a serious attempt to listen to yourself, that is, to reread the paper with the goal of making it clear and concise.

Having used my writing as an example in the first chapter, I have chosen samples of writing for this chapter that are not my own. (They are drawn from drafts of papers written by my students and colleagues.) After discussing six types of revision, I end the chapter with a list of questions you should ask yourself as you sit down to edit your paper.

REVISING FOR CONTENT

Does each sentence say something? Every sentence in your paper should make a point; your reader should not have to ask why you included it. Consider the following examples drawn from student papers:

Alcoholism is a social problem.

In history people witnessed and practiced punishment for many centuries, and people today still exercise it.

Between 1820 and 1860, this country experienced changes economically, socially, politically, and territorially.

Are you surprised to learn that alcoholism is a social problem, that the history of punishing criminals is longstanding, or that the United States changed in several ways in the 1800s? The emptiness of these sentences is striking. Such statements of the obvious severely weaken a paper; they require a simple editorial response—deletion. Begin from scratch by writing a new sentence that says something.

Vacuous sentences are likely to appear in introductions or conclusions to papers or at the beginning or end of paragraphs. In these places, you may attempt to summarize what you are about to write, or what you have written. In attempting to say too much, you may end up saying nothing. (On the other hand, in *drafting* your paper, don't be afraid to say the obvious. Saying the obvious may help get you going. But when the time comes to revise, cut out such stuff.)

REVISING FOR CLARITY

Will your imagined readers find your sentences clear? A reader should not have to labor through your paper, stopping to figure out what you had in mind when you wrote a particular sentence. Here are several things to keep in mind as you revise your paper for clarity:

1. Sometimes clarity is obscured because of poor word choice. Take, for example, the following sentence:

```
There is a distinct relationship between the socializa-
tion and selection of group members.
```

To state that there is a "distinct" relationship between two things doesn't tell us much. By substituting a more precise adjective, the sentence now makes a clear point:

```
There is an inverse relationship between the socializa-
tion and selection of group members.
```

We might go one step further and revise the delayed opening ("There is . . .") of this sentence, and, in the process, eliminate a few words.

```
The socialization and selection of group members are in-
versely related.
```

2. Avoid weak intensifiers, such as *very, really, actually,* and *certainly*. Instead, choose words that express your thoughts clearly and accurately. Thus, if something is "very important," why not

describe it as "decisive," "essential," or "indispensable"? What is the difference between *"actually* being cured" and "being cured," or between *"really* confident" and "confident"? These words are fine in everyday conversation, but they aren't much help in writing social science papers.

3. Vague quantitative references often signal a need to revise for clarity. These are a particular problem in social science writing when counting is important to the story being told. In reporting that

```
Most respondents agreed that single women should be able
to obtain an abortion.
```

the obvious question arises—or ought to arise, when you read with an eye toward revising—as to how many are "most"—a little over half? two-thirds? nine-tenths? You can clarify this finding by substituting a more exact term for most, or you can explain what you mean by most. Here are two possible revisions:

```
Two-thirds of the respondents agreed that single women
should be able to obtain an abortion.
```

```
Most respondents (67%) agreed that single women should be
able to obtain an abortion.
```

In the reporting of research findings, words such as *several, many, most, majority, few, some,* and *minority* should usually be either avoided or explained. If, however, you are discussing results that are also reported in a table, you can safely rely on these more general terms; interested readers can look to the table for more specific information.

4. Problems of clarity may also stem from poor organization of a sentence. Particularly in long sentences, make sure that phrases that go together are placed alongside one another.

```
Three groups, each with a different motive and goal, led
the crusade toward determinate sentencing: prisoners,
professors, and politicians.
```

A reader might anticipate some modification of "determinate sentencing" after the colon, but instead finds the "three groups" that are referred to at the beginning of the sentence. Why wait until the end of the sentence to identify these principal actors? Rewriting, we have

```
Three groups—prisoners, professors, and politicians—
each with different motives and goals, led the crusade to-
ward determinate sentencing.
```

If the sentence, though clearer, now seems excessively wordy, we might revise further:

```
Prisoners, professors, and politicians—each with dif-
ferent motives and goals—led the crusade toward determi-
nate sentencing.
```

5. Ambiguous use of the pronouns *it, they,* and *them* can produce unintended and sometimes comic meanings. In a paper on halfway houses, a student wrote

```
Structuring them as closely as possible to a normal home
setting has helped the mentally ill adjust to the environ-
ment outside of the hospital.
```

No doubt the author intended *them* to refer to halfway houses, but as this sentence is written, she is "structuring" people ("the mentally ill"), not buildings. In revising, a simple substitution of "half-way houses" for "them" takes care of the confusion.

Here is an example in which *they* leads to similar problems of ambiguity:

> Although roughly equal numbers of men and women work in white-collar occupations, they are more likely to report greater job satisfaction.

Who are happier at work, men or women? When revising, make sure that your reader can easily identify who or what you have in mind when you use *it, they, them, these, those.* Even if it sounds a bit awkward, it is better to repeat whatever *it* is than to create potential ambiguities.

REVISING FOR CONCISENESS

Does each sentence make its point in the fewest words possible? Revising for content and clarity makes sure each sentence says something; revising for conciseness makes sure what you say is said well. Wordiness is probably the most common problem I find in papers I edit. It is undoubtedly my own worst writing problem. (By the way, in an earlier draft the previous sentence read: "I know that it undoubtedly is the worst problem in my own writing.") Long sentences are not necessarily wordy, but they are often candidates for editorial dissection. Consider this sentence from a paper on the birth of the asylum in America:

> Definitions of social deviance, as well as ideas as to what the treatment of social deviants should be, differed greatly between the Americans of the Colonial period and those of the Jacksonian period, causing the treatment of these people to change dramatically.

Is the author saying that as ideas about treating deviance changed, deviants were treated differently? (Note that the vague reference to "these people" at the end of the sentence is also troubling.) It would be clearer (and obviously shorter) to write the following:

> Definitions of social deviance differed greatly between the Colonial and Jacksonian periods, resulting in a major change in how deviants were treated.

Revision may also be warranted when too little is said in too many sentences. If a series of brief statements appears repetitive, there is a good chance that a revised version with fewer sentences will leave a stronger impression. Discussing the deinstitutionalization of mental patients, a student writes as follows:

> Deinstitutionalization has its roots in three philosophical ideas. These all relate to the way in which mentally ill people can be treated most effectively and humanely. These three concepts are: normalization, treatment in the least restrictive setting, and the developmental model of programming.

The tedious repetition of "these" in the second and third sentences ought to warn the writer that revision is in order. One such revision might be this:

> Deinstitutionalization is rooted in three philosophies—normalization, treatment in the least restrictive setting, and the developmental model of programming—each of which seeks the most effective and humane treatment of the mentally ill.

Although the revised sentence is relatively long, it avoids the repeated reference to the "three philosophies." One could, of course, divide it into two sentences:

```
Deinstitutionalization is rooted in three philosophies—
normalization, treatment in the least restrictive set-
ting, and the developmental model of programming. Each of
these seeks the most effective and humane treatment of the
mentally ill.
```

Passive constructions should usually be edited out; they add words and often obscure who or what is the intended subject of the sentence. In a passive construction, the subject does not act but is acted upon. "The respondent was interviewed by the researcher" is passive. (The subject of the sentence—the respondent—is acted on.) In contrast, "The researcher interviewed the respondent" is active. (The subject of the sentence—the researcher—acts.) Consider the following two sentences alongside their possible revisions:

```
PASSIVE: With regard to sentencing, women criminals
are treated more favorably than their male counter-
parts.
ACTIVE: The courts give lighter sentences to women
than to men.
PASSIVE: It was for the benefit of the handicapped
children that the law was brought into effect.
ACTIVE: Congress created the law to benefit handi-
capped children.
```

In the first example, the subject—women criminals—is being acted upon by the (implied) judicial system. In the second, "the law" is likewise acted upon by some unspecified legislative body. By using active constructions, the revisions of these two sentences state unambiguously who or what is acting.

The example about sentencing illustrates another common source of wordiness: elaborate phrasing of simple terms. Does it make sense to write "male counterparts" instead of "men"? Social scientists have long been criticized for inventing a language to describe everyday life in complicated terms, and expressions like "male counterparts" only add fuel to the critics' fire. So do phrases such as "socialization process" (socialization *is* a process) or "individual norms" (norms are standards established and recognized by *groups*). This does not mean that you should avoid social science terminology altogether. Some examples of their appropriate use are discussed in the following section on "Revising for Trite Expressions and Social Science Jargon."

Consider one last example that combines many of the problems we have been looking at. Returning to the paper from which the last sample sentence was drawn, we read the following:

```
Now that it has been discussed whether the nonhandicapped
students will have adverse reactions to the mainstreaming
process, those who are directly affected by the Act must
be considered.
```

There are at least four ways in which this sentence can be improved through revision. First, the author is obviously trying to make a transition from one section of the paper to another, but she uses a passive construction to do so ("Now that it has been discussed . . ."). Second, the vague diction of the sentence obscures its meaning. *Are* nonhandicapped students adversely affected by mainstreaming? If they are not (and that is her point), isn't it better to say, "Nonhandicapped students are not adversely affected by mainstreaming"? Third, the sentence is plagued by wordiness. "Mainstreaming process" is used where "mainstreaming" would suffice, and "those who are directly affected by the Act" is a needlessly complicated synonym for "handicapped children." Fourth, the sentence ends with another passive construction ("those . . . must be considered"). Searching for a clear and concise path out of this mess, we might revise the sentence in the form of a question:

```
If mainstreaming does not adversely affect nonhandi-
capped students, how does mainstreaming affect the handi-
capped?
```

The phrase "Now that it has been discussed" is one of several "academic passives" (Barnet and Stubbs, 1986:383) that crop up in scholarly writing. Most academic passives are some variation on "It has been found/demonstrated/discussed/argued/shown" or "In this paper it has been found/demonstrated. . . ." Don't thrust the responsibility for what you write onto the paper itself; instead, identify the source. If you are the one "finding, demonstrating, or showing," simply write "*I* found," "*I* demonstrated," or "*I* showed." If others deserve the credit, name them: "The instructor found, "Cloward and Ohlin (1966) argued. . . ." Acknowledging the source of each statement will help you avoid passive constructions and unintentional plagiarism at the same time.

REVISING FOR TRITE EXPRESSIONS AND SOCIAL SCIENCE JARGON

Trite Expressions

Does any sentence contain trite expressions? In contrast to sentences written in the passive voice, which often convey a sense of pretentious formality, trite phrases make your writing too familiar. They also cloud intended meanings. What do the authors of the following sentences have in mind?

```
Not all juvenile delinquents go on to pursue a life of
crime.
```

```
Telephone interviewing is a quick and dirty way to collect
survey data.
```

What does the author of the first sentence mean by "a life of crime"? Is she saying that most juvenile delinquents grow up to be lawful citizens? That most juvenile delinquents (who, as a group, commit more serious crimes) fail to become adult offenders (who, as a group, commit more serious crimes)? That most delinquents are not recidivists? Similarly, what does the second author mean what she describes telephone interviewing as "quick and dirty"? Does she mean that it is "inexpensive," "expedient," or "efficient"? Or is she suggesting that telephone interviewing produces less reliable or less valid information than other methods of data collection? As they are written, it is impossible to know what the creators of these sentences intended to convey to their readers.

Jargon

Does any sentence contain jargon: social science terms used vaguely or incorrectly? Some social science terms have been incorporated into everyday language and, in the process, have lost their precise and intended meanings. When authors of social science papers misuse such terms, their writing suffers. Two of the most frequently misused social science terms appear in the following sentences:

```
Due to the bureaucracy of the organization, I was unable
to obtain the average age or average length of employment
for each group of workers.
```

```
The fieldwork experience left me feeling quite alienated.
```

The word *bureaucracy* has a specific meaning in the social sciences; it refers to organizations with hierarchical structures of authority in which relationships among members are based on position and in which formal rules dictate how things are done. In the first example, the author uses *bureaucracy* to mean the ways in which members shift responsibility to others, making it difficult to obtain information (i.e., equivalent to the everyday expression "red tape"). At least this is what I *think* she means. Without identifying exactly what aspect of bureaucracy created the problem, the statement is ambiguous.

In the second example, it is almost impossible to decipher the author's intention in describing her experience as "alienating." An informed reader might first ask *what* the writer is alienated from (work, others, or self?) and then wonder what dimension of alienation the writer has in mind (powerlessness, meaninglessness, isolation?) In short, concepts such as alienation and bureaucracy have firmly established meanings in the social sciences; to use them casually reveals a lack of understanding of these meanings. (Another frequently misused concept is "charisma." Students often describe someone with a dynamic and captivating personality as "charismatic." As a social science concept, it refers to a type of authority or leadership ability based on a person's extraordinary personal characteristics.)

Does this mean that you should always delete social science terminology from your writing? Certainly not. When properly used, technical terms can be word-saving devices, allowing you to write clearly and concisely. Consider the following observations:

```
Acquiring a peculiar vocabulary is often essential to how
individuals learn to think and behave in accordance with
group values and norms.
```

What if the author had instead written the following:

```
Acquiring a peculiar vocabulary is often an essential as-
pect of socialization.
```

Students of sociology know that *socialization* may be defined as "how individuals learn to think and behave in accordance with group values and norms." The writer knows that they are familiar with the meaning of "socialization," and so she uses the word, in the interest of conciseness. The revision preserves the meaning of the original sentence and does so in considerably fewer words.

One final note: Don't blame *society* for everything. Whenever I read through a stack of student papers or examinations, I am overwhelmed by the power of *society* to shape human behavior: "Society encourages people to want things they can't afford"; "Society is responsible for our drug problem today"; "Society rewards conforming behavior." Although (to paraphrase Emile Durkheim) society is obviously more than the mere sum of its parts, don't fall into the habit of reifying it. Used indiscriminately, *society* becomes a vehicle for sloppy social science writing (and thinking).

As you reread a sentence that contains the word *society,* ask yourself: Whom or what do I mean by *society?* Quite often, you can replace *society* with a more specific subject: "Advertisements encourage people to want things they can't afford"; "People take drugs to avoid the responsibilities of everyday life"; "Parents and teachers reward conforming behavior among children." If you remember to state your observations concretely, you will become a better analyst of social life. At the same time, you will spare your reader some confusion.

REVISING FOR SPELLING ERRORS

Is every word spelled correctly? Edit with a dictionary at your side, or use a word processor with a dictionary program. If you don't own one, buy a dictionary the next time you are in your college bookstore. (Look for *Webster's Collegiate Dictionary, Webster's New World Dictionary,* or *The American Heritage Dictionary*.) Papers submitted without having been edited for clarity and conciseness pose problems in and of themselves; misspelled words magnify these shortcomings. Your reader may be sympathetic to your difficulty in presenting ideas using the correct words, as long as whatever words you choose are at least spelled correctly. But if your paper reveals that you have not even bothered to check the spelling of a word, you will probably lose your reader's goodwill.

Although all of us have words we seldom spell correctly, many students find the following words particularly troublesome:

INCORRECT	CORRECT
devient, devience	*deviant, deviance*
respondant	*respondent*
defendent	*defendant*
signifigant, signifigance	*significant, significance*
socialogy	*sociology*
indispensible	*indispensable*
questionaire	*questionnaire*

enviornment	*environment*
bureacracy	*bureaucracy*
Gemeinshaft, Gessellshaft	*Gemeinschaft, Gesellschaft*

Notice that the first six words in this list contain the *schwa*—the unstressed vowel that sounds like "uh." Such words are often difficult to spell because of the ambiguity of which vowel sounds like "uh." Is it "indispens*i*ble," "indispens*e*ble," or "indispens*a*ble?" Don't guess; look up words like these until you are sure which vowel is correct.

Your instructor will probably be annoyed if you misspell terms that are discussed in course materials. If an instructor corrects your spelling on one paper, don't make the mistake of misspelling the same word on later assignments. In particular, always check the spelling of proper nouns. There is only one *b* in Max Weber's name; Goffman's first name is *E*rving, not *I*rving; Alexis *de* Tocqueville, not Alexis D'Tocqueville, wrote *Democracy in America*. Your instructor may not expect you to memorize the spelling of every term or individual mentioned in a course, but misspelling important words on a class assignment gives the impression that you have not bothered to check the accuracy of your class notes.

REVISING FOR GRAMMAR AND PROPER WORD USAGE

Because a comprehensive discussion of editing for grammatical errors would easily fill a third of this book, I will mention only one recurrent problem in student papers I read—run-on sentences and comma faults. For a detailed examination of subject–verb agreement, parallel construction, punctuation, and other matters of grammar, I suggest you consult these excellent references: Barnet and Stubbs (1986), Maimon et al. (1981), Strunk and White (1979), Zinsser (1976). Complete citations for these books are given in the References at the back of this book. After discussing run-on sentences, I focus on four examples of proper usage that require particular attention.

1. *Run-on sentences and comma faults.* Run-on sentences result from writing as though you do not need punctuation to separate

independent clauses; comma faults (or comma splices) occur when you decide that a comma (or semicolon), rather than a period, will correct the problem of writing run-on sentences.

Run-on sentence:

```
Richardson's (1955) methodology has been challenged how-
ever no one has replicated his study.
```

Comma fault:

```
Richardson's (1955) methodology has been challenged,
however no one has replicated his study.
```

Be on the lookout for run-on sentences and comma faults in sentences that contain transitional words (e.g., *however, instead, nevertheless, consequently,* and *thus*) or in long sentences of any kind. Following the advice of Barnet and Stubbs (1986), you have at least five options in revising these grammatical mistakes:

a. Use a period to separate the two independent clauses into two sentences.

```
Richardson's (1955) methodology has been challenged. No
one, however, has replicated his study.
```

(Note that I have placed *however* after *no one* in the revision to emphasize the contrasting information of the second sentence. This does, however, affect the grammatical solution I suggest.)

b. Use a semicolon.

```
Richardson's (1955) methodology has been challenged; no
one, however, has replicated his study.
```

c. Use a comma and a coordinating conjunction (e.g., and, or, not, but, yet).

```
Richardson's (1955) methodology has been challenged, yet

no one has replicated his study.
```

d. Use a subordinating conjunction (e.g., although, because, unless, when, after), and make one of the independent clauses subordinate to the other.

```
Although Richardson's (1955) methodology has been chal-

lenged, no one has replicated his study.
```

e. Change one of the independent clauses to a word or phrase. (Note that I have altered the subject of the first clause in making this revision.)

```
Richardson's (1955) study has been challenged on method-

ological grounds but not replicated.
```

2. *Which/that.* These two words are not interchangeable. *Which* introduces a nonrestrictive clause, an idea or some information that is not essential to the meaning of the sentence. *That*, in contrast, begins a restrictive clause, one that, if omitted, changes the meaning of the sentence.

```
Schools that disregard federal guidelines for recruiting

minority students are denied government funding.
```

```
This school, which disregarded guidelines for recruiting

minority students, was denied government funding.
```

The first sentence narrows or restricts the subject from "schools" to a certain group of schools—"schools that disregard federal guidelines." That is, it defines under what conditions schools are denied funding; the meaning of the sentence is changed dramatically if the restrictive clause beginning with *that* is removed (i.e., "Schools are denied government funding"). In the second sentence, in contrast, the subject is now narrowed or restricted. The subject is simply "this school." The sentence retains its original meaning if the nonrestrictive clause beginning with *which* is omitted (i.e., "This school was denied government funding"). The nonrestrictive clause does, however, provide additional information about the particular school that was denied funding.

Notice that in the second sentence the clause beginning with *which* is set off by commas. Whenever a clause contains a parenthetical remark or an aside (and therefore must be set off by commas to make sense), use *which*.

3. *Effect/affect.* As a noun, *effect* means *result:*

```
The interviewer's sex had an effect on the response to
this question.
```

Effect as a verb means *to bring about:*

```
The interviewer's sex effected a change in the response to
this question.
```

Affect is usually used as a verb meaning *to influence:*

```
The interviewer's sex affected the response to this ques-
tion.
```

Sometimes, particularly in psychological writing, *affect* is used as a noun meaning *feeling, emotion,* or *desire:*

```
Although child abuse is a highly emotional issue, the sub-
jects showed little affect in discussing it.
```

4. *i.e./e.g.* Don't confuse i.e. (an abbreviation for the Latin *id est,* "that is") with e.g. (an abbreviation of *exempli gratia,* "for

example"). Use i.e. when you provide another way of saying something you have written; use e.g. to give one or more illustrations of something you have written. Here are two examples in which i.e. is appropriate:

> We selected respondents using a systematic random sam-
> pling technique, i.e., beginning with a random start, ev-
> ery fifth person was selected from a list of all community
> residents.

> No one involved in the research (i.e., professors, con-
> federates, or subjects) anticipated the results of the
> simulated prison experiments.

In the first example the independent clause following i.e. provides detailed information about what the author means by "a systematic random sampling technique." In the second example, the parenthetical phrase specifies precisely who the author had in mind when writing "no one." In both sentences, the words preceding i.e. and those following i.e. are equivalent; they could have been switched without changing the meaning of the sentence.

When your goal is to illustrate rather than restate, use e.g. Here is an example in which e.g. is used appropriately:

> Typologies depicting changes in the dominant forms of
> social organization (e.g., Toennies's <u>Gemeinschaft</u> and
> <u>Gesellschaft,</u> Marx's "feudal" and "capitalistic,"
> Maine's "status" and "contract") are an important part of
> the intellectual tradition of the social sciences.

Toennies, Marx, and Maine were not the only social theorists who described the changes in collective life associated with the passing of the Middle Ages. The student might well have added Durkheim, Weber, Redfield, Cooley, and Parsons to the list following e.g. These additional references, however, are not necessary; the information following e.g. is meant to be illustrative, not exhaustive. You simply want to give your reader a better idea of what you are talking about by using a few well-chosen examples.

What if, in an effort to convey a sense of the quantity of available illustrations, the author had written this sentence instead? (The only change is the addition of "etc.")

```
Typologies depicting changes in the dominant forms of so-
cial organization (e.g., Toennies's Gemeinschaft and Ge-
sellschaft, Marx's "feudal" and "capitalistic," Maine's
"status" and "contract," etc.) are an important part of
the intellectual tradition of the social sciences.
```

Because the list of examples following e.g. is understood to be only partial, adding etc. (an abbreviation for *et cetera,* "and so on") is inappropriate. Moreover, placing etc. at the end of a few examples, rather than giving the reader a sense that the author can supply additional examples if asked to do so, often has the opposite effect; it leaves the reader with the impression that the author has nothing in mind. In general, avoid *etc., and so forth,* and *and so on.* If you have something to add, say it. If you don't, place a period at the end of the sentence and go on to the next one. In either case, you won't leave your reader wondering what information you might have added.

5. *Data. Data* is the plural of *datum:* a piece of information or something known. When you write papers in the social sciences, you will use the word *data* quite a lot; you will probably never use the word *datum.* Always pair *data* with a plural verb (e.g., "the data *are* consistent," "the data *were* interesting," "these data *have* never been challenged").

THE BIG PICTURE: REVISING THE PAPER AS A WHOLE

If you follow these suggestions for revision, your paper should be full of sentences that are relatively meaningful, clear, concise, and free of spelling and grammatical errors. But, as you know, an effective paper is more than a collection of several pages of effective sentences. To reap the benefits of sentence-by-sentence revision, you must think seriously about how those sentences can be used to build strong paragraphs and, in turn, a strong paper. Before you turn in your paper, review this list of issues that address revisions of your paper as a whole. (By its nature, this type of revising cannot be illustrated on a sentence-by-sentence basis. I therefore refer you to previous sections of this book for help in making revisions that concern the paper in general.)

1. *Beginnings*. Does your introduction accurately and clearly state the thesis of your paper? Introductions and conclusions are critical elements of any paper. Your readers will expect the first few paragraphs of your paper to tell them, briefly and in an organized way, what will follow. Try to capture your reader's interest with your introduction—begin with an interesting example or analogy, or tantalize your reader by hinting at your conclusions—but at the very least, present the major issues you address in your paper (see Chapter 3).

2. *Endings*. Does your conclusion do more than summarize your paper? Use the conclusion of your paper to go beyond a restatement of your thesis ("In this paper I have shown X, Y, and Z"). Demonstrate the broader significance of your argument by providing analogous illustrations; suggest some questions that remain unanswered by your analysis; or emphasize the novel approach or interpretation you have made in your paper. Be certain, however, that you set the stage for your concluding remarks; the conclusion of your paper is no place to introduce entirely new arguments or evidence (see Chapter 3).

3. *Organization*. Does your paper tell a logical story, that is, does it move in an orderly way from one point to another? Is similar information grouped together, or is it scattered throughout your paper? One way to improve the organization of a paper is to write from an outline (see Chapter 4), but often you can improve a paper's organization by simply asking about each sentence (after the first): Does this sentence follow from the previous sentence? If so, how does it follow it?

4. *Consistency*. Is the tone of your paper consistent? If you begin your paper using formal language, do you maintain that tone? Is your choice of verb tense consistent; for example, if you

have been describing your research methodology in the past tense, do you present your results using the same tense? Do citations to research materials follow a consistent format? (See Chapter 7 on citation form.)

5. *Balance.* What is the balance between description and analysis in your paper? Most social science papers are analyses, and you should devote more time to analysis than to description. Do you have enough evidence to support the points you are making, or do you have too much evidence? In a qualitative analysis based on interview data, for example, two carefully selected quotations from respondents are preferable to five quotations that provide redundant evidence for the same point. Finally, what is the balance between quotation and summary in your paper? Is every quotation well chosen and important to your analysis? (See Chapter 4, and Chapter 7 on when and how to use quotations.)

6. *Emphasis.* Are the major points of your paper clearly distinguishable from the minor points? If your paper is sufficiently long, consider using subheadings to divide it into major sections (see Chapter 4). Emphasis can also be established by repetition or summary; returning to an issue a few times in your paper demonstrates its significance to your reader.

7. *Transitions.* Does your paper include proper transitions (e.g., "furthermore," "on the other hand," "however") as you move from one paragraph or one point to another? Is it clear when you are making a point of comparison or contrast? Well-placed transitions minimize the choppiness of your writing and strengthen an analysis employing comparisons (e.g., "similarly," "in addition to," "moreover") or differences (e.g., "nonetheless," "although," "in contrast").

PUTTING IT ALL TOGETHER: AN EDITOR'S GUIDE

Here is one guide I have found helpful in structuring the editing process. Although it is written as a set of questions directed toward "the author," you should be able to use this guide when revising your own work as well as that of others.

An Editor's Guide*

1. *Statement of Thesis*— Read the opening of the paper (the title, the first sentence, the first paragraph). Is the introduction effective? Does it grab your attention and also let you know where the author is going? If so, explain (in the margin) what makes it good. If not, suggest a possible improvement.

What is the author's thesis? Is it clear? Does it seem immediately reasonable? If the thesis does not seem reasonable, was the writer astute enough to realize this, and to assure you that he or she would go on to make it reasonable?

2. *First Time Through*— Finish reading the paper. Does the author support a consistent thesis or are several ideas competing for attention? Jot down your impressions after this first reading. On balance, was the paper well written? Also make a note of any major mechanical or stylistic weaknesses you found troubling.

3. *Second Time Through*— This time consider the following questions as they apply to each paragraph:

—What is the main point of this paragraph?

—Is the main point easy to find?

—Is the main point reasonable?

—Does the author provide adequate evidence for each argument? Are there adequate details and examples? Are there paragraphs needing more development or support?

Look at the transitions (e.g., "therefore," "on the other hand," "furthermore") both BETWEEN paragraphs and also WITHIN them. Are more transitions or more accurate transitions needed? Are the kinds of transitions all the same or do they vary?

Is the CONCLUSION effective? If so, explain what makes it good. Are there loose ends in the argument, which need to be tied up? Is the conclusion anticlimactic? If so, suggest a possible improvement.

4. *Third Time Through*— On this last reading look for two things: tone and style.

Does the author know his or her audience? Does he or she maintain a consistent, credible tone throughout? Is the level of dic-

---

*This guide draws heavily from one developed by members of The Writing Program, UCLA.

tion (not only word choice but also sentence structure) consistent with the dominant tone?

Concentrate on those mechanical or stylistic problems you found particularly distressing. Consider such things as grammar (punctuation, subject–verb agreement, etc.), spelling, wordiness, use of parallel structure, and other stylistic matters that make the essay difficult to read. Mark at least two representative sentences that require revision, and suggest ways to revise them.

Use this guide as a flexible standard, modifying it to serve your needs best. You will have to identify fairly quickly the major problems of the paper and focus your efforts there. Similarly, if you are editing a long paper, you would edit one section or subsection of the larger piece at a time. It would not make sense to edit a fifty-page paper in the manner outlined here. Above all, seek to combine some elements of sentence-by-sentence editing with some attention to overall revisions—rethinking or restructuring—of any paper you edit.

References

Alaska Statehood Commission. 1982. *More Perfect Union: A Preliminary Report of the Alaska Statehood Commission.* Juneau: Alaska Statehood Commission.

Barnet, Sylvan, and Marcia Stubbs. 1986. *Barnet and Stubbs's Practical Guide to Writing.* Boston: Little, Brown and Company.

Becker, Howard S. 1963. *Outsiders: Studies in the Sociology of Deviance.* New York: The Free Press.

————. 1986. *Writing for Social Scientists.* Chicago: University of Chicago Press.

Cuba, Lee J. 1984. "Reorientations of Self: Residential Identification in Anchorage, Alaska." Pp. 219–237 in *Studies in Symbolic Interaction,* Vol. 5, edited by Norman K. Denzin. Greenwich, Conn.: JAI Press.

Gerth, H. H., and C. Wright Mills, eds. 1976. *From Max Weber: Essays in Sociology.* New York: Oxford University Press.

Grob, Gerald N. 1972. "Review of *The Discovery of the Asylum* by David J. Rothman." *Political Science Quarterly* 87:325–326.

Homans, George C. 1950. *The Human Group.* New York: Harcourt, Brace and Company.

Hummon, David M. 1986. "Urban Views: Popular Perspectives on City Life." *Urban Life* 15:3–36.

Kanter, Rosabeth Moss. 1972. *Commitment and Community.* Cambridge, Mass.: Harvard University Press.

Kitsuse, John I. 1962. "Societal Reaction to Deviant Behavior." *Social Problems* 9:247–256.

Lofland, Lyn H. 1985. *A World of Strangers: Order and Action in Urban Public Space.* Prospect Heights, Ill.: Waveland Press.

Maimon, E. P., G. L. Belcher, G. W. Hearn, B. F. Nodine, and F. W. O'Connor. 1981. *Writing in the Arts and Sciences.* Cambridge, Mass.: Winthrop Publishing.

McCormick, Albert E. Jr. 1977. "Rule Enforcement and Moral Indignation: Some Observations on the Effects of Criminal Antitrust Convictions upon Societal Reaction Processes." *Social Problems* 25:30–39.

Melbin, Murray. 1978. "Night as Frontier." *American Sociological Review* 43:3–22.

Miller, Joanne, and Howard H. Garrison. 1982. "Sex Roles: The Division of Labor at Home and in the Workplace." *Annual Review of Sociology* 8:237–262.

Pillemer, Karl. 1985. "The Dangers of Dependency: New Findings on Domestic Violence Against the Elderly." *Social Problems* 33:146–158.

Schuman, Howard, Charlotte Steeh, and Lawrence Bobo. 1985. *Racial Attitudes in America: Trends and Interpretations.* Cambridge, Mass.: Harvard University Press.

Strunk, William, Jr., and E. B. White. 1979. *The Elements of Style.* New York: Macmillan.

Suttles, Gerald D. 1968. *The Social Order of the Slum: Ethnicity and Territory in the Inner City.* Chicago: University of Chicago Press.

Sykes, Gresham M., and David Matza. 1957. "Techniques of Neutralization: A Theory of Delinquency." *American Sociological Review* 22:664–670.

Vaughan, Diane. 1986. *Uncoupling: Turning Points in Intimate Relationships.* New York: Oxford University Press.

Wells, Miriam J. 1984. "The Resurgence of Sharecropping: Historical Anomaly or Political Strategy?" *American Journal of Sociology* 90:1–29.

Williamson, John B., and Kathryn M. Hyer. 1975. "The Measurement and Meaning of Poverty." *Social Problems* 22:652–653.

Yarrow, Marion Radke, Charlotte Green Schwartz, Harriet S. Murphy, and Leila Calhoun Deasy. 1955. "The Psychological Meaning of Mental Illness in the Family." *Journal of Social Issues* 11:12–24.

Zinsser, William. 1986. *On Writing Well: An Informal Guide to Writing Nonfiction.* New York: Harper and Row.

Index